ALAN SILLITOE:
A CRITICAL ASSESSMENT

Alan Sillitoe:
A Critical Assessment

STANLEY S. ATHERTON

W. H. ALLEN · LONDON
A Howard & Wyndham Company
1979

*Printed and bound in Great Britain by
Butler & Tanner Ltd, Frome and London
for the Publisher, W. H. Allen & Co. Ltd,
44 Hill Street, London W1X 8LB*

ISBN 0 491 02496 7

Contents

Preface

This study of Alan Sillitoe focuses on the work which made his reputation, the novels and stories in which he invoked the conditions, attitudes and ethical perspectives of working-class life in a unique and comprehensive manner to offer a fresh vision of contemporary society. It examines a number of relevant criteria, including the social and political background, biographical material, the author's views on the nature and function of literary art, the place of a working-class frame of reference in the tradition of the English novel, and independent sociological evidence to provide an assessment of Sillitoe's early work. It also offers an appraisal of more recent work and points to the directions Sillitoe has taken since moving away in the late sixties from a purely working-class perspective.

Footnotes have been kept to a minimum in the interests of the general reader, but full documentation is included in the bibliography which follows the text to satisfy the needs of specialists.

Acknowledgements

I would like to express my gratitude to all those who have assisted in the preparation of this study, and in particular to Alan Sillitoe, who has been especially generous with his time, with access to both published and unpublished material from his files, and with his superb coffee; to Dr Howard German, who suggested the need for such a book and offered useful and sympathetic advice on the early chapters; to Dr J. K. Johnstone, who with patient encouragement provided scholarly criticism of an earlier version of the manuscript; to Anthony Burgess, Ruth Fainlight, Adelheid Fandrey, Professor Judith Kennedy, Michael Sillitoe, and my family, who helped in a variety of ways; to the editors of *The Dalhousie Review* for the opportunity to publish a preliminary study of Sillitoe's work; and finally to St Thomas University, Fredericton, Canada, for granting sabbatical and special leave which made the research and writing of this book a good deal easier than it might have been.

For permission to quote I would like to thank Mr Sillitoe and his publishers, W. H. Allen, as well as the following sources:

Chatto and Windus and Richard Hoggart for permission to quote from *The Uses of Literacy* by Richard Hoggart; Robson Books Limited for permission to quote from *Big John and the Stars* by Alan Sillitoe; Martin Secker & Warburg Limited for permission to quote from *The Culture of Cities* by Lewis Mumford; Dr F. Zwieg for permission to quote from his works, *The British Worker* and *Labour, Life and Poverty*, both published by Penguin Books Limited; Routledge & Kegan Paul Limited for permission to quote from Madeline Kerr's *The People of Ship Street* and from David Downes' *The Delinquent Solution: A Study in Subcultural Theory*; A. M. Heath & Company Limited and Mrs Sonia Brownell Orwell for permission to quote from *The Road to Wigan Pier* by George Orwell, published by Martin Secker & Warburg Limited; Kildare Dobbs and the Canadian Broadcasting Corporation for permission to quote from 'The Sounds of Criticism' – an essay for radio.

List of Illustrations

Between pages 80 and 81

Chapter One

The Temper of the Times:
Introduction and Background

On the fifth day of July, 1945, British voters elected for the first time a Labour Government with a majority in the House of Commons. It was led by Clement Attlee, a public school old boy and Oxford graduate who had 'immersed himself in a movement and in the life of a totally working-class locality at a time when the Labour Party, far from being a vehicle for political ambition, had still to be formally created'.[1] It seemed to some contemporary observers such as R. B. McCallum and Alison Readman in *The British General Election of 1945* that a revolution had taken place, albeit an orderly British one, and that inequalities and antagonisms of class would quickly disappear as the new government exercised its powers to make Socialism a practical reality.

It soon became apparent, however, that the millennium was not at hand. Britain had been financially devastated by the war effort, and any economic and social changes would have to be brought about under extremely unfavourable conditions. The temporary mood of elation and triumph created by victory and the Labour landslide at the polls quickly turned sour. Rationing continued almost unaltered, queuing became a way of life, and in 1947, during the worst winter in twenty-five years, a severe shortage of coal led to a national fuel crisis. Hugh Dalton, then Chancellor of the Exchequer, called the crisis in his volume of memoirs entitled *High Tide and After* 'the first really heavy blow to confidence in the Government and in our post-war plans. .... Never glad, confident morning again.'

Despite growing rumblings of disillusion and discontent, the first post-war government achieved a good deal of Socialist legislation. Most controversial, perhaps, was the nationalisation of key industries, including coal, electricity and gas (and later iron and steel), and the means of transport, including road haulage, railways and canals. Debatable though the legislation was, it was desirable to Labour, according to C. F. Brand in his history of the party, 'not as an end in itself, but as a useful tool both for planning high productivity and for a better distribution of wealth and greater social equality.' Greatly expanded social services were also planned to reduce the divisions between classes. A National Insurance Act was introduced, comprising a new compensation act which was to provide for insurance in the case of lost income through accident or illness, and an act making provision for old-age pensions. A National Health Service came into being which nationalised the hospitals, provided free medical services and free drugs. And corporation-owned housing was encouraged and supported to offer inexpensive accommodation to low income families. The Welfare State, based on the assumption that the less economically fortunate should share the freedom from worry of other classes about the necessities of life, had come into being.

In the meantime the nation was having a difficult time paying its way. The development of the Cold War was accentuated by the Communist takeover of Czechoslovakia in 1948, and the concomitant costs of rearmament put new strains on the economy. The distintegration of the colonial network meant reduced access to important raw materials for industrial development, and, as the war against Communist guerillas in Malaya illustrated, what Empire was left was becoming more costly to administer. By 1949 Britain was faced with the humiliation of a devalued pound, and in 1951 she lost her most valuable foreign investment, the Abadan oil refinery, to Iranian nationalisation.[2]

By the early fifties, increasing numbers of Englishmen were becoming aware that the war had signalled the end of an era and an attitude. Temporarily impoverished, shorn of an Empire, the island nation was being forced into a markedly reduced position of power in international affairs. To the generations who had known imperial glory, powerfully represented in the nation's leadership, such a position was as difficult to accept as the need for radical changes in the tradition-bound social structure at home. Yet to many the change was welcome, for sensitive Englishmen had long felt the guilt of Empire and were happy enough to see India and other former colonies go their own way. A new sense of national identity was being formulated that had little place for nostalgia, and the literature of the fifties was to reflect its development.

Coronation year, 1953, marked a kind of watershed in post-war British literature. The fiction of the forties had managed with few exceptions to ignore the changing attitudes of large numbers of intelligent Englishmen towards their hierarchical social system and their growing sense of confusion about the nation's political future. While the finest novel of the decade, Malcolm Lowry's *Under the Volcano* (1947), did offer a telling symbol of the dying past in the alcoholic person of Geoffrey Firmin, ex-public school boy, ex-naval officer and ex-British consul abroad, it was essentially a subjective vision rather than a representative expression of social upheaval. There was of course noteworthy non-fictional evidence of anti-establishment attitudes in the success of Stephen Potter's Gamesmanship books, which offered a caricature of class stratification by satirising displays of social superiority, and in Ronald Searle's corrosive St Trinian's cartoons, which pilloried the class-oriented public school system.

With the publication of John Wain's novel *Hurry on Down* in 1953, a new kind of hero was born. Knowledgeable, well-brought up, the beneficiary of a state-supported university education, Charles Lumley recognises the anachronism of traditional class identification-badges and makes an attempt to get beyond definition by class. He becomes in turn a window-washer, smuggler, hospital orderly and chauffeur. Then, after a brief stretch as a night-club bouncer, he satisfies both himself and society by joining a group of script writers for a well-known comic. His signature, however, is his protest, his willingness to rebel actively against a social structure he feels is no longer viable.

For the first time since the war a dissatisfied generation could identify with a contemporary fictional hero. Among specific reactions the novel provoked was an essay competition on class in the *Observer*. One of the winners, Margaret Maison, summed up her contribution forcefully on December 27: 'Our system of class distinction in Britain is as unpardonable and indefensible as our attitude towards it. It is an outrage and we dote upon it, it is a canker and we glory in it, it is a captivity and, bound fast in the shackles of tradition, we hug our rusty chains.' A number of the other winning entries echoed Miss Maison's ironic tone of dissent.

The following year provided fresh evidence that the shackles of tradition were rapidly becoming less constraining. A trio of promising new writers – Kingsley Amis, William Golding and Iris Murdoch – published first novels in 1954, and one of them, Amis's *Lucky Jim*, became an immediate popular sensation. Its hero, Jim Dixon, had strong links with Charles Lumley, as Kildare Dobbs has shown persuasively in *Reading the Time*: his background was proletarian, his politics leftish and his attitudes fresh and iconoclastic, and his sallies against sham, pretence and hypocrisy quickly captured the public imagination. As an assistant university lecturer he was in a fine position to snipe at various forms of establishment pomposity, and despite the perils to his career this involved, he took great pleasure in doing so. As a result Lucky Jim quickly became a cult figure, coupled in the public mind with growing resentment against hereditary privilege and social posturing. So widespread was his popularity, in fact, that for the rest of the decade he was to remain a touchstone of popular culture.

If fiction had begun to capture the mood of social ferment

in the early fifties and thus to connect with a large general public, drama had not as yet done so. London's West End theatre was moribund. There were few playwrights who were authentically post-war, and those who had begun to write before the war offered little that was exciting. Apart from imports such as Beckett's *Waiting for Godot*, the British stage was mainly occupied by middle-class drawing-room comedy with mildly sexual overtones, melodramatic who-dunnit plays and the inevitable and mostly forgettable musicals, as more than one drama critic of the period pointed out. Of course there were a few notable exceptions: T. S. Eliot and Christopher Fry championed verse drama in the late forties, most memorably with *The Lady's Not for Burning* and *The Cocktail Party*, while J. B. Priestley, Noel Coward and Terence Rattigan continued to produce box-office successes.

John Osborne's *Look Back in Anger*, first produced on May 8, 1956, at London's Royal Court Theatre, offered something new. Timely and socially committed, the play made an immediate impact. Impressed reviewers attempted to communicate the excitement of the new work (*The Times* was a notable exception); and a brief extract shown on television resulted in capacity crowds for the remainder of the original short run and two revivals within the year. To a generation convinced by *Lucky Jim* of the validity of protest, Jimmy Porter's stinging and eloquent indictment of a complacent Britain was an expression of political and social righteousness. Essentially they were rebelling against an attitude, a persuasive nostalgia for the past that denied the expression of a more realistic national consciousness. They shared a feeling that while the nation continued to look back with longing, the individual could only experience confusion and frustration. Jimmy Porter knew that his personal revolt, through marriage and mistreatment of a member of the class which he felt was responsible for the situation, was an impotent gesture of defiance. But for a generation that rejected class privilege, and had lost confidence in the traditional leadership of a social and political Establishment, the gesture seemed worth making. And the Government's bumbling ineptitude over Suez and morally ambiguous stand on the Hungarian Revolution in the same year gave strength to their convictions.

Nancy Mitford's *Noblesse Oblige* (1956), a study of upper-class shibboleths, offers an intriguing footnote to the social ferment Osborne was documenting in his drama. Its core was a linguistic study by a philologist named Alan Ross which suggested that Englishmen could be divided into two classes by their speech: U or Upper-class and non-U or others. The work became a best-seller, and one result of its popularity was widespread recognition that the mystique of tradition-ally superior classes was now openly being questioned from within, for the Honourable Nancy Mitford was very much a U person. Before long a growing number of Englishmen would begin to look on the aristocracy merely as proprietors of tourist attractions in the stately-homes business, and after this the upper classes could never be quite the same.

Nonetheless the privileges of position were still strong – and there were many young Englishmen who felt that one way to relieve the frustration and confusion they felt was to force their way into the economic élite. John Braine's novel, *Room at the Top* (1957), traces the fortunes of such a man. Joe Lampton, the ambitious youthful protagonist, covets the wealth, position and power his working-class birth had not given him. His carefully calculated moves take him from the back-to-backs of his native Dufton to marriage with the daughter of a successful Yorkshire industrialist. But in the effort to gain the world of Susan Brown, 'the girl with the Riviera suntan', and the Aston Martin, fine home and luxurious life she represents, Joe Lampton loses his humanity and his soul. He alienates his relatives, causes a woman who loves him to commit suicide, and at the end of the novel takes refuge in drunkenness from a self he has come to despise.

James Lee, in his study of Braine's work, suggests that 'de-spite Joe's calculated and callous actions he is not simply a villain – for Braine intends us to see Joe's plight as that of the young man who can rise in no other way than by wooing the Establishment.' Such an interpretation is somewhat mis-leading, for in this novel the Establishment is being strategically infiltrated rather then wooed. This timely appeal to contemporary social dissent, and the perennial English fascination with hypergamy, helped to make the novel an outstanding commercial success. But there were those, including Frank Hilton writing in *Encounter* in February, 1958, who felt that Braine's novel was additional evidence of a sick society where people like Joe Lampton merely moved 'out of the class they were born into ... [to land] in a social limbo where everyone else is an enemy.' Echoing Jimmy Porter, Hilton also asked his countrymen: 'Are we sick of ourselves – are we sick of Britain, the Britain we're supposed to be, the first-rate power that we're not, the great little island no one ever allows us to forget we once were, with our mouldering Few and our scrapbooks for 1928, and our Agincourts and our Trafalgars and our gallant retreat from Dunkirk and all the crazy, bewildering jingo junk we call our heritage...?' Anthony Crosland, expanding on the problem two years later in the *Spectator* (February 12, 1960), called the continued existence of an 'exceptionally rigid class structure, with its deep social and cultural divisions' a unique British phenomenon. He went on: 'Upon this rigid structure we have now imposed a (limited) degree of upward social mobility through the educational system. The result is a direct confrontation of social classes, notably at Oxford and Cambridge, on a scale not previously known: and out of this confrontation sometimes comes an understandable explosion of class resentment, sharper than in other countries precisely to the degree that the social contrasts were initially more marked.' (It now seems ironic that within ten years of the Labour government's increase in state scholarships for university attendance, an awareness of the social and individual problems brought about by a conflict between longstanding class prejudices and more democratic educational opportunities had become a mark of the contemporaneity of English creative writing, but it is nonetheless true.)

In spite of mixing in the universities and occasional infiltration by Joe Lamptons, the middle and upper classes in England remained largely ignorant even in the mid-fifties of working-class conditions, attitudes and aspirations. It was generally assumed, for instance, that the road to Wigan Pier had been travelled a long time ago, and that the advent of the Welfare State had more or less emancipated the working-class from poverty. A number of sociological studies conducted during the decade showed otherwise. From Ferdynand Zweig's *Labour, Life and Poverty* (1948), to Richard Hoggart's *The Uses of Literacy* (1957), examinations of working-class life indicated a series of sharp contrasts between the workers and those more comfortably situated. Michael Young and Peter Willmott's *Family and Kinship in East London* (1957), for example, showed that attitudes to work, education, family and home differed markedly from those of higher social classes. J. M. Mogey described the working-class interest in the immediate and specific and the tendency to let the future take care of itself in *Family and Neighbourhood* (1956). B. M. Spinley in *The Deprived and the Privileged* (1953), and R. M. Titmuss's *Essays on 'The Welfare State'* (1958) both found working-class family relationships dependent on a series of peculiar and difficult economic situations. And Richard Hoggart made frequent reference to the conflicting values of middle and working-classes, of *them* and *us*.

These studies, along with the drama of Osborne and other working-class playwrights such as Arnold Wesker (*Chicken Soup With Barley*, 1958, and *Roots*, 1959), represented a world whose interests, loyalties and values differed greatly from those of the stately home or even the comfortable semi-detached of the new suburban developments. And Wesker's commitment to what G. S. Fraser called 'evangelical Socialism' went far beyond his drama. In the late fifties he formed an organisation known as Centre 42 to bring good drama to working-class audiences in the provinces who would not normally have access to it, and also founded a theatre in an abandoned London railway roundhouse to promote drama by and about the working-class. But sociological studies are usually not widely read and new plays, unless they are in some way unusual, are seen by relatively few. There was still no talented novelist equipped by experience to bring home the contemporary conditions and aspirations of working-class life to a wider public. With the publication of *Saturday Night and Sunday Morning* (1958), however, and *The Loneliness of the Long-Distance Runner* a year later, it was obvious that the working-class had found a brilliant spokesman.

If there is such a thing as fate influencing publication of the efforts of untried novelists, Alan Sillitoe's literary début in the late fifties is an example of its operation. The times were certainly propitious. Growing public reaction against smug complacency had become evident in the sympathetic reception given the work of a number of new young writers, even extending to a rather turgid philosophical study of alienation by Colin Wilson entitled *The Outsider* (1956). The world of the gentleman no longer dominated literature, or life either for that matter, as William Van O'Connor pointed out in *The New University Wits* (1963). The significant figures now included heroic solitaries making their rebellious way through a resisting world, doing their individual best to break up an ossified social structure. Life could no longer be seen by the writer as a luminous halo, a comfortably protective transparent envelope insulating the protagonist from social concern and commitment. The feel of the fifties was captured instead in titles such as *Look Back in Anger* and *Declaration*, a collection of insurrectionary credos by a number of well-known young writers edited by Tom Maschler, and *The Angry Decade*, Kenneth Allsop's study of the contemporary social and literary milieu, and in the actions and attitudes of characters like those in Alan Sillitoe's novels.

Sillitoe's first two protagonists fall into a recognisable pattern of dissent. Arthur Seaton, a Nottingham factory lathe-operator, and Smith, a Borstal long-distance runner, are related through their proletarian origin, alientated stance and active condemnation of social and political institutions to Charles Lumley, Jim Dixon and Jimmy Porter. But Sillitoe's characters have an additional dimension through their consistent adherence to a class-oriented code of values which gives direction and motive to their actions. They exhibit, for example, an anti-authoritarian bias that goes beyond rejection of the establishment for strictly individual reasons and becomes an aggressively working-class expression of grievances. Their awareness of this representative role gives their social commentary a strong, even at times savage, incisiveness which in turn reflects the crusading zeal for social reform felt by Sillitoe himself at this point in his career. At the same time their expression is a rejection of a long-standing attitude towards class problems, for as Dennis Potter observed in *The Glittering Coffin* (1960), 'talking about class in highly personal terms is [traditionally] a shocking and embarrassing thing for an Englishman to do; there is a kind of pornography about the subject, an atmosphere of whispered asides and lowered eyes.'

Broadly speaking, Sillitoe's early working-class fiction may be divided into two groups. The first includes the novels *Saturday Night and Sunday Morning* and *Key to the Door* (1961), the novella *The Loneliness of the Long-Distance Runner* and about twenty short stories. The second consists of the first two novels of a trilogy, *The Death of William Posters* (1965), and *A Tree on Fire* (1967). Within the first group, *Saturday Night and Sunday Morning* and *Key to the Door* may conveniently be called the Seaton saga, for along with a number of the short stories they chronicle the lives of the Seaton clan in and around industrial Nottingham. *The Loneliness of the Long-Distance Runner* and most of the short stories also deal with the underprivileged working-class to which the Seatons belong. The emphasis in this early fiction is on the conditions and allegiances of working-class life, presenting an honest and unsentimental account which is highly critical of the existing social order and the seemingly unbridgeable gulf between the two worlds of *them* and *us*. In this work the seeds of the dissent which colours much of Sillitoe's fiction may be found. The first two novels of the trilogy are carefully built on the foundations of the earlier fiction, though they transpose working-class heroes into alien surroundings. The more positive emphasis here is on social reform, on changing the world of *them*. Both Frank Dawley, a guerilla fighter, and Albert Handley, an anarchistic artist, are dedicated to the creation of a utopian society. Their attempt to bring it about is drawn from a conviction they share with earlier Sillitoe protagonists – a willingness to do battle for values they believe are right and to go on fighting even though the short-term odds are overwhelmingly against them.

Sillitoe's novels and stories published after 1967 are not so easily classified. There was a long break, for example, before the third novel of the trilogy, *The Flame of Life*, was published in 1974. In the meantime his work had become less vocal in its condemnation of social injustice and had moved towards a more muted expression of the need for social reform. And there was an increasing emphasis on the suffering experienced by particular individuals as a result of society's hostility or indifference. That is to say, while Sillitoe still recognised the need for social reform, he had begun to explore and present the problem in a different manner. Yet despite a shift in focus in later work, there can be little doubt of the continuing force and impact of the early novels and stories. The social ferment of the fifties in Britain encouraged a literature of questioning and revolt. Sillitoe's early use of the cultural allegiances and ethical perspectives of working-class life to illuminate important areas of this discontent should be tentatively considered as one of the more significant literary achievements of the period.

Notes and References

[1] See D. J. Heasman, ' "My Station and Its Duties" – The Attlee Version,' *Parliamentary Affairs*, 21 (Winter 1967–68).
[2] For the selection and arrangement of material illustrating the state of the nation in the decade and a half following the war, I am indebted to 'The Sounds of Criticism', an essay for radio by Kildare Dobbs, presented on the Canadian Broadcasting Corporation's FM network between March 18 and April 15, 1966, and subsequently published in a condensed version as the first chapter of *Reading the Time*.

Chapter Two

An Individual Record:

Sillitoe's Apprenticeship to his Craft

Alan Sillitoe was born on March 4, 1928, at 38 Manton Crescent in the Lenton Abbey estate of council houses rented to low income families by Nottingham Corporation. The family had been associated with Nottinghamshire for some generations, and had established a tradition of sturdy, if perilous, independence. On his father's side the antecedants were urban, on his mother's, rural. His paternal grandfather, Frederick Sillitoe, had been born in Wolverhampton in 1853, and came to Nottingham with his wife Ada (née Blackwell) as a master upholsterer in the eighteen-seventies. After working for some years for a large firm, he set up on his own at the corner of Trafalgar and Wyville streets in Radford. For the rest of his life he earned a precarious living for his family of six sons and two daughters, reputedly spending the time when there was no work breeding birds in an aviary at the top of the house. Sillitoe's maternal grandfather, Ernest Burton, born in 1866 near Lenton, worked for most of his life in the village as a blacksmith in the forge he had inherited from this father. He married a local girl of Irish descent, Mary Ann Tokins, and she bore him eight children, three boys and five girls.

Christopher Sillitoe, Alan's father and the fifth son of Frederick and Ada, was born in Radford in 1902. At the age of twenty-two he married Sylvina Burton. Because of a long series of childhood illnesses, he never learned to read or write, and remained throughout his life 'a man with neither craft nor calling, a labourer who was often unable to find any work at all.'[1] So it was that during the difficult years of the thirties, when there was little work to be had, he was frequently unemployed. It was then that Alan, along with his brothers Brian and Michael and sisters Peggy and Pearl, knew real hardship. Alan later recalled 'the day in 1934 when I went to meet my father from work at the tannery. He opened his pay packet, took out the twenty-eight shillings and threw the envelope into the canal, where it floated away, the last pay packet he handled until 1939.' Lack of money meant that it was nearly impossible to provide even the basic necessities of food and shelter. At times the children were dependent for food on the local dinner centre, where they were given a hot meal once a day. And the family was forced to move six times in almost as many years because of disputes with slum landlords over rent. Finally a more-or-less permanent home was found at 5 Beaconsfield Terrace, a short street backing on to the Raleigh Bicycle factory, where the Sillitoes continued to live until Christopher's death in 1959.

Against this background of constantly threatened home life, school offered the Sillitoe children a kind of stability. At first young Alan found it 'a mystifying appendage to life, a bewildering world of wooden building blocks, cold swimming baths, Punch-and-Judy shows, and instruction in reading, writing and telling time.' But by the time he was eight the boy had become an avid student. A number of years later he reminisced in an article for *Education* how 'learning began to fascinate me and draw me in. Wanting to learn all I could set me in the forefront of the A streams from then on.' His scholastic interests proved to be eclectic. History and geography were fascinating no matter who taught them. He became intrigued by coastlines, mountain ranges and foreign names, and spent long hours reading and making maps, assiduously developing an interest in topography that was to become a lifelong passion. When he was ten, stirred by a radio serialisation of *Les Misérables*, he began to teach himself

French with the aid of an old Pitman's grammar. English, on the other hand, needed the stimulus of a good instructor. While spelling tests and finding new words made it interesting, he hated studying grammatical rules. Yet of all the teachers Sillitoe had at school, he remembers best a man whose name was Charles Rowe, known affectionately to the children as 'Titch', who taught him English and encouraged his early attempts at writing.

In September, 1939, he was evacuated to Worksop, twenty-seven miles from Nottingham. But after three months his parents brought him home, convinced (as it turned out, rightly) that no matter how long the war went on, Beaconsfield Terrace was in little danger of being bombed. His failure to pass the notorious eleven-plus examination despite two attempts, possibly in part the result of interrupted schooling, kept him out of grammar school and condemned him to Radford Boulevard School for boys. It was there that he first became aware of the escapist possibilities of romantic fiction. Encouraged to read regularly by a few helpful teachers, he began to devour adventure stories, working his way through the works of Hugo and Dumas, Scott and Stevenson, Marryat and Conan Doyle, Rider Haggard and R. M. Ballantyne. Sillitoe feels that his family's poverty also stimulated his interest in fiction because 'going to the pictures on Saturday afternoons . . . was such a rarity and marvel that I began to make up my own cinema shows. Left to entertain my brothers and sisters I told stories aloud to keep them quiet. I was in such demand at the age of ten that I soon ran out of plots, so I turned to books for guidance.' The story-telling sessions were to last for another four years, enriched in the final year or so by vivid recreations of the thieving exploits of his marauding cousins in their brief periods of freedom from gaol and military service. Sillitoe's own memories of this period in his life are substantiated by his younger brother Michael, who recalls with great affection the countless hours he spent listening fascinated to Alan's stories of escape, adventure and intrigue.

The interests of the boy suggest the passions of the man;

and young Alan's preference for certain subjects at school reflects his first awareness of the discrepancy between the actual and the possible. The areas of learning in which he chose to interest himself offered a series of substitutes for the bitter necessities of working-class existence. In retrospect Sillitoe has suggested that his boyhood reading 'was the only means of going into a world other than the one around me, one which I often found disagreeable because it was too close, and sometimes too alien.' The quest for more perfect worlds which informs much of his later fiction had its genesis in this childhood discovery of imaginative alternatives that could transcend the harsh realities of the Nottingham slums.

At the age of fourteen Sillitoe followed an established working-class pattern and left school. His elder sister Peggy was already employed in a sweet factory, and although he envied the eleven shillings and sixpence she brought home each Friday night, he was reluctant to leave his studies. But the family needed money, and so in the late spring of 1942, wearing clogs and a new pair of overalls, he went to work in the Raleigh Bicycle factory. For nearly three months he put in nine hours a day on piece-work. His first job was 'burring', 'sitting at a bench with a sharp chisel or screwdriver and chipping away brass burrs that remained on a piece of work, before it went to the nearby polishers.' That first week he took home thirty shillings, turned it over to his mother, and was given half a crown for spending money. Soon after this he was promoted and became the operator of a stand-up drill. Before long, however, he got involved in a dispute with the foreman over the rate he was paid for his work. Finding himself unable to earn what he considered a reasonable wage from his new job, he gave notice, establishing his independence by talking a number of his 'mates' into leaving with him. For the next eighteen months he worked in a plywood factory owned by the A. S. Toone Company, helping to make jacquard mechanisms for weaving lace. Then, finding the work boring, he became a capstan lathe operator with a small engineering firm called Firman's, a position he kept until his army call-up in 1946.

The undemanding routine of his work soon stifled any imaginative faculty he had begun to develop, and the creative schoolboy was quickly submerged in the hedonistic young factory worker. Recalling these years later in an interview, Sillitoe remembered them as 'a good time; I worked a lot but it was a good time, going out with girls, having no cares, money for the first time in my life.' On VJ Day, at the age of seventeen, he left Nottingham for the first time on a day-return ticket to London. His reaction on arrival reveals the limitations three years of factory life had imposed on his vision: 'It seemed an unreal town, and because I didn't see engineering works lining the Mall, and factories along Oxford Street, and back-to-backs on Hyde Park, I was rather contemptuous of it, and assumed that London didn't have any factories at all.' Yet the trip did reawaken his old interest in geography; and, with the prospect of more extensive travel ahead, he was a willing volunteer to the Royal Air Force the following May. In the meantime he had joined the Air Training Corps as a cadet, partly because social pressure dictated that all working boys become involved in the war effort, partly to satisfy a need to become better educated than he was. The training he received in the ATC in mathematics and elementary navigation, among other things, led to his acceptance for pilot's training by the Fleet Air Arm in the spring of 1945. But the end of the war with Japan meant that no more aircrew would be needed, and his call-up was deferred. A year later he began training as a wireless operator with the RAF.

After training he was given an AC2 rating and sent on the troopship *Ranchi* to Singapore on May 8, 1947, exactly a year after his call-up. He was to stay in Malaya, at Butterworth in Province Wellesley, for the next two years, operating a direction-finding (D/F) station. He found the work interesting to the point where he considered becoming a ship's radio operator after his national service was over. And he enjoyed the relative isolation and freedom of the communications hut, where he worked alone and rarely had to wear a uniform. He also had a great deal of time for reading during his stay in Malaya, and it was here that he became acquainted with Robert Tressell's *The Ragged Trousered Philanthropists*, a novel about working-class life in Edwardian times which he found both enlightening and intellectually stimulating. On August 23, 1948, he left for England on the *Dunera*, carrying with him the memories that were to furnish much of the experience recorded in his third novel, *Key to the Door*. At Blackpool a demobilisation medical test revealed that he had contracted tuberculosis abroad, and he was sent to an Air Force hospital at Wroughton, near Swindon in Wiltshire, to recuperate.

In the next sixteen months at the sanatorium Sillitoe developed a prodigious appetite for reading. During the 'enforced retirement from life, and to absorb the shock of it', he read several hundred books. His boyhood interest in romantic adventure was now superseded by a calculated desire to educate himself. Accordingly he began with the Greek and Latin classics in translation and then systematically worked his way through the canon of great writers. He found a particular affinity with Fielding, Tolstoy and Stendhal, as well as with Melville and Emily Brontë. More recent novelists whose work he found compelling include Hardy and Conrad, Bennett, Lawrence, Hasek and Camus.

Stimulated by the word-magic of these masters, Sillitoe began to write himself, at first exploring the possibilities of language in poetry, then committing to paper an account of his Malayan experiences. He tried writing short stories, many of which were incorporated in his later fiction and one of which later formed the basis of his novel, *The General*. Late in 1949, at the age of twenty-one, he attempted his first novel. The entire work, one hundred thousand words entitled 'By What Road', was completed in seventeen days, and Sillitoe claims to have been genuinely surprised when his neatly-typed manuscript was returned with a letter of rejection from a major publisher. But by this time he had given up his plan to become a ship's radio operator and decided to apprentice himself seriously to the craft of writing. In December of 1949 he was released from hospital, and after six weeks' leave was discharged from the Air Force with a disability pension of forty-five shillings a week. Throughout the next year he stayed in Nottingham, living at home and spending much of his time sitting in the Nottingham Reference Library writing short stories, including 'Uncle Ernest', and working on 'The Deserters', a novel he has yet to publish. It was then that he met the woman he was to marry, an American-born poet named Ruth Fainlight who was living in the city with her husband. In the spring of 1951 Sillitoe spent two months at a cottage near Aylsham in Kent owned by his aunt, a sympathetic woman who had brought up five coal-miner sons. In June he moved to nearby Hastings, where Ruth was staying. For the next six months he abandoned fiction altogether and wrote only poetry, addressed mainly to Ruth. Then, on January 10, 1952, they left for France on the Newhaven–Dieppe ferry. On his passport he defined himself as a writer.

During the next six years the couple lived on the continent, first in France in an unfurnished stone cottage on the olive-covered hills behind Menton and later in Spain, their only income the RAF pension and a twenty-six-shilling-a-week National Health allowance. He wrote steadily, even though money was so scarce that at times he could not afford paper. In fact, one short story called 'Canning Circus', which was later incorporated into *Saturday Night and Sunday Morning*, had to be written on the backs of book jackets. Determined to continue writing nonetheless, he completed a second novel while staying at the cottage. Entitled 'The Man Without A Home', it was never published.

In January of 1953, Sillitoe travelled from France to Majorca with a friend named John Tarr and a pet ginger cat called Nell, which he smuggled into Spain in a shoebox. He was later joined there by Ruth, and settled into a small house in Soller to write. For the next five years he worked regularly, often putting in a ten-hour day, turning out stories, novels and poems but publishing little. On occasion, when the writing was not going well, he taught English and Ruth worked for a villa-letting agency to supplement their meagre income. Yet there were also intensely productive periods, such as the winter of 1953–54, which was spent expanding an earlier short story about the conflicting interests of art and war into the novel which was eventually published, much revised, as *The General*. At the same time he was redrafting a mass of material in a manuscript provisionally called 'Letters From Malaya' and published in 1961 as *Key to the Door*. In 1954, with the encouragement of Robert Graves, with whom he had become friendly during the previous summer, Sillitoe began to shape a novel about Nottingham from a number of stories and sketches he had already completed. A manuscript list compiled that year groups sixteen stories totalling sixty thousand words 'on the same theme'. A chapter by chapter plan prepared about the same time shows that nine of these stories, including 'Once in a Weekend', which was to give the novel its memorable opening sequence, were used in the new work, tentatively called 'The Adventures of Arthur'. Further drafts followed, and by 1955 the novel had acquired the title under which it was to be published, *Saturday Night and Sunday Morning*. It was not until August, 1957, however, that it was finally completed to Sillitoe's satisfaction. Even then five publishers rejected it before W. H. Allen decided, in their own words, 'to take a chance on it'. By this time, spring of 1958, Sillitoe had returned to England after a two-month stay in Alicante on the Spanish mainland, during which time he had completed the first half of a brilliant new story, 'The Loneliness of the Long-Distance Runner'. Notice of the acceptance of *Saturday Night and Sunday Morning*, along with a hundred pound advance, reached him at Brighton, where he and Ruth were visiting her parents.

He had already published a small collection of poems entitled *Without Beer or Bread* in a limited paperback edition, and had had a children's story, 'Big John and the Stars', included in an anthology. Now, on the strength of greater expectations, he decided to move to London. After four weeks in a Dulwich flat he settled for a time in Camden Town in a room-and-kitchen combination which he remembers as being so squalid it had to be completely whitewashed to provide a minimum of cheer. Yet the stay in Camden Town is memorable for Sillitoe for a better reason: it was here that he completed *The Loneliness of the Long-Distance Runner*, justly considered one of his finest works. In January, 1959, a three hundred pound advance from Knopf, his American publisher, allowed him to take a lease on a small beamed cottage in Whitwell, Hertfordshire. He stayed there for more than a year, preparing *The General* for publication and continuing work on *Key to the Door*. On November 19 he and Ruth were married.

In the meantime his work was receiving critical recognition. *Saturday Night and Sunday Morning* was judged the most promising first novel of 1958, and Sillitoe received a silver-mounted quill from the Authors' Club in London. Then in May, 1960, he was surprised and awed to hear that *The Loneliness of the Long-Distance Runner* had won him the coveted Hawthornden Prize, a prestigious award given annually for the best piece of imaginative writing by an author under forty. The same year W. H. Allen released *The Rats and other poems*, a collection of thirty-three short lyrics, including ten published in *Without Beer or Bread*, and the title poem of 942 lines. Apart from *The Rats*, which exhorted the individual to resist conformist pressures of civil servants, organisation men and other bureaucrats (collectively known as rats), the collection exhibited little originality. It is noteworthy, though, as an early statement of a theme which is much in evidence in Sillitoe's later work, his insistence on the integrity of individual response in a world which seems bent on destroying it. Most of the remaining year was taken up with preparation of the screenplay for the film version of *Saturday Night and Sunday Morning*. Directed by Karel Reisz and starring Albert Finney as the hero, Arthur Seaton, and Shirley Anne Field and Rachel Roberts as the two women in his life, it was both a critical and a commercial success. But Sillitoe had found the work of recasting the novel for the screen exhausting, and after the film's première in October he spent nearly five months on holiday in Tangiers.

Returning to London in the spring of 1961, he took a lease on the flat in Notting Hill Gate which he was to keep for the next four years. During the spring and summer he worked at a new screenplay, this time for *The Loneliness of the Long-Distance Runner*, and made the final revisions to *Key to the Door*. The autumn was devoted to poetry and shorter fiction. In March, 1962, his son David was born; and six weeks after his birth Sillitoe's restlessness caused the family to leave London once again for Tangiers. For the next year he travelled throughout Morocco, beginning a new novel entitled *The Death of William Posters* and working intermittently on some of the short stories that were later collected and published in *The Ragman's Daughter and Other Stories*. In the meantime the film version of *The Loneliness of the Long-Distance Runner* was released. Directed by Tony Richardson and starring Tom Courtenay and Sir Michael Redgrave, it received an enthusiastic response from critics and public alike. Then, early in 1963, an invitation from the Soviet Writers' Union to visit the USSR coincided with a sudden longing for London, and after a year of 'paradise and timelessness' Sillitoe returned to England.

In April and May he spent a month travelling extensively in the Soviet Union, and later in the year he spent four weeks in Czechoslovakia. Settled again in the Notting Hill Gate flat for the winter, he recorded the former experience in an intensely personal account entitled *Road to Volgograd*. It was published in 1964. In the tradition of the best travel literature, the book is highly idosyncratic, revealing as much about the writer himself as about the territory he describes. Early in the first chapter Sillitoe warns the reader that he will be going around 'like an old-fashioned traveller, with an eye for topography', and much of the time he does just that, compiling a geographer's rhapsody on the confluence of earth, sky and water on a grand scale. Even the cityscapes – Stalingrad-Volgograd, Leningrad and Irkutsk – are described with cartographic precision, so that it comes as no surprise when Sillitoe stands fascinated in Lenin's rooms before a map of Petrograd showing 'a campaign street plan of the October rising worked out by the Military Committee. All strategic points were marked, all lines of advance from factories and barracks, to converge on the centre and the Winter Palace.' The incident itself is unremarkable, but it lingers in the reader's memory, perhaps because it underscores some of the central interests in Sillitoe's life – his fascination with military strategy and with guerilla tactics in particular, and his passion for topography and cartography – which give a number of his novels and stories their characteristic flavour.

A number of reviewers were baffled and irritated by Sillitoe's largely uncritical account of Soviet lifestyles in *Road to Volgograd*. Yet if one recalls the deprivations of his childhood, when his own family suffered real hardship and the state seemed unwilling or unable to pay attention to their needs, his enthusiasm for what seemed on short acquaintance to be a workers' paradise is understandable. On a number of occasions in the book he remarks on the apparent classlessness in Soviet life, and is at pains to point out a pervasive sense of community in which Soviet citizens refer to themselves as 'we' rather than as 'them' and 'us'. Despite this eagerness to praise Soviet attitudes, however, *Road to Volgograd* is not a political treatise. On the other hand, its emphasis on political and social interaction helps to bring Sillitoe's passion for travel into perspective. His dissatisfaction with England, largely based on the conditioning of his working-class background, has motivated him for many years to search after more ideal social situations abroad. The urge to travel, to escape physically from a society whose hierarchical traditions and reactionary attitudes he has always found unpalatable, is a natural extension of his schoolboy desire to escape imaginatively from the Nottingham slum. *Road to Volgograd* is perhaps best seen as the record of one such escape.

In April, 1964, a stage version of *Saturday Night and Sunday Morning*, adapted for the theatre by David Brett, was produced at the Nottingham Playhouse. Truncated and episodic, its effect weakened by the amplified incursions of a pop guitar group, it received poor reviews and soon closed. The pattern was to be repeated in London two years later when the play had a short run in the West End at the Prince of Wales theatre. In 1964 Sillitoe also published a new collection of poetry entitled *A Falling Out of Love and other poems*. Though most of the thirty-nine poems included in the volume were undistinguished, critics pointed to a more controlled, disciplined use of images than had been evident in *The Rats*. Late in the year, after spending the spring with Robert Graves in Majorca and holidaying in Scandinavia during the summer, Sillitoe decided to resettle in Spain. For the next four years he divided his time between a permanently-rented home in Deyà and a house he had bought in Clapham. In 1965 he published a major new novel, *The Death of William Posters*. The first in a projected trilogy, it traced the activities of a working-class man, Frank Dawley, who leaves his family and the Nottingham slum and factory life he has known for twenty-seven years and moves into new worlds, socially and geographically. Critical reaction, though mixed, was generally favourable, and there was little evidence of the go-back-to-Nottingham-Mr-Sillitoe attitude so much in evidence in 1960 when he published *The General*.

Sillitoe spent most of the following year working on the second novel of his trilogy, entitled *A Tree on Fire*, in which Frank Dawley's harrowing experiences as a freedom fighter with the Algerian FLN are recounted in painstaking detail. At the same time he continued to write poems, completing a number on the twin themes of love and death with a view to publishing a more unified group of poems than he had in previous collections. And with Ruth Fainlight as co-author he completed his first stage script, an adaptation of a play by the Spanish writer Lope de Vega entitled *All Citizens Are Soldiers*. For diversion he worked on a children's story about the adventures of a country cat in the city for the first time. In 1967 *A Tree on Fire* and the children's book, now called *The City Adventures of Marmalade Jim* and illustrated by Dorothy Rice, were both published. The former, like *The Death of William Posters*, was the cause of mixed critical reaction, characterised in this case by praise for Sillitoe's uncanny ability to make the desert battle scenes come convincingly alive and by reservations about his over-abundant use of metaphor and a tendency to weigh his hero down with too much philosophical speculation. The children's book was well received.

In 1967 Sillitoe visited the Soviet Union twice, partly in an attempt to use up some of the non-exportable roubles credited to him as royalties on Russian translations of his work. In June he travelled by car through Scandinavia to Leningrad, motored south to visit Moscow and Kiev, and returned to the West by way of Rumania and Yugoslavia. In France on the way home he made a point of visiting some of the more important battlefields of the Great War, collecting impressions which found their way into a number of his later books. While he was away *All Citizens Are Soldiers* had a brief run at the Theatre Royal, Stratford East, beginning on June 20. The play was directed by William Martin and staged by a group of young actors who called themselves 'The 1520 Contemporary Theatre Company'. It closed after a few performances. In September Sillitoe flew to the Soviet Union, once again travelling as an ordinary tourist. He was there when Ilya Ehrenburg died, and attended the writer's funeral. A few days later he responded to an invitation to speak at the Gorki Literary Institute, and took for his subject the freedom of writers to say what they liked without fear of incurring official displeasure. As a tourist Sillitoe was free to say what he liked, though he recalls that his speech was not popular with the authorities.

In November, 1967, he left for the south of France accompanied by his family. They stayed at Le Tholonet, near Aix, until March, when they moved on to Majorca to spend four months at Torre Susaina in a house loaned to them by Robert Graves. During the winter Sillitoe worked on a play entitled *This Foreign Field*, which he had begun earlier, and also finished the last of the forty-four poems he was to include in *Love in the Environs of Voronezh* for publication in the spring. In May he wrote 'Mimic', one of his finest stories, in seven days, and before returning to England he finished a number of others for a new collection entitled *Guzman, Go Home* to be published in the autumn. Back in London he happened by chance to see a new American film entitled *Counterpoint*, the end result of his having sold the film rights to *The General* some years before. Directed by Ralph Nelson and starring Charlton Heston and Maximillian Schell, it bore only superficial resemblance to Sillitoe's novel. Except in France, where it was acclaimed, it was a critical and a box-office failure.

Late in the year he was invited by the Union of Soviet Writers to visit Russia on the occasion of the hundred and fiftieth anniversary of Turgenev's birth. It was a short trip – within two weeks he had left for home – and it was destined to be his last to the Soviet Union for the foreseeable future. He was finding the Russian government's treatment of writers, and of certain minority groups such as Jews, increasingly distasteful, and he realised that any public statements he might make at home on these matters would be severely compromised by continued visits to the Soviet Union.[2]

Throughout 1969 Sillitoe stayed in England, spending most of his time working on a long picaresque novel entitled *A Start in Life* for publication the following year. Unlike many writers who become proficient as novelists, Sillitoe still finds the short story a challenging and rewarding genre, and in breaks away from working on the novel he continued to produce new ones, including at least two which he would publish in his next collection. In July he purchased a large Edwardian vicarage along with two acres of land in the tiny village of Wittersham in Kent. Strategically located a short distance from Lydd airport and a number of seaports, yet only a two hour drive from London, it seemed to offer an ideal base from which to travel abroad without at the same time being inconveniently far from his publishers and the amenities of the capital. At Christmas Sillitoe took his family on holiday to the south of Spain, where they spent two months at Frijiliana, near Nerja.

Most of 1970 was taken up with preparing a film script for *The Ragman's Daughter* and working on a Utopian fantasy entitled *Travels in Nihilon*. In March *This Foreign Field* was produced at the Roundhouse in London by the Contemporary Theatre Group, and was also directed by William Martin. The play, a study of class and conflict between generations, was largely ignored by the critics and consequently drew small audiences. It ran for only a few days. A happier reception was given Sillitoe's new novel, *A Start in Life*. Not only was it admired by most critics, but it very quickly became a popular success. Those who still had reservations about Sillitoe's departure from the working-class milieu he had depicted so admirably in earlier fiction were disarmed by the new work. A contemporary picaresque in the manner of Fielding's *Tom Jones*, it not only showed Sillitoe's ability to turn one of the most traditional of genres to his own ends, but it also revealed a well-developed, robust sense of humour which up to this time many critics had felt he lacked. It was impossible to ignore the fact that *A Start in Life* was brilliantly funny in a wide range of comic modes, from slapstick and farce to satire and literary parody.

Nineteen seventy-one was the year of the census, a memorable one for Alan Sillitoe. Believing that government bureaucrats had no right to pry into his private affairs, he took a strongly individualist position and refused to answer more than three hundred questions on the form. He did list his age as a hundred and one to show the enumerators, as he remarked in an essay on the episode, 'that I wasn't born yesterday'. Despite increasing pressure from the authorities over a period of time, he remained firm in his conviction and refused to complete the form. The end of the matter came seven months later when an unrepentant Sillitoe appeared before a magistrate and was fined £25 with costs, an event which *The Times* laconically reported to its readers the following morning.

In June he spent an agreeable week in Finland as a guest of Finnair and his publisher in Helsinki, and in July he motored with his family to Bellagio, near Lake Como in northern Italy, to visit friends. He also collaborated that summer with Ruth Fainlight and Ted Hughes, a close friend, to produce a limited edition of *Poems*. Brought out by the Rainbow Press, it was a sumptuously produced volume printed on linen paper and handbound in gold-embossed leather binding. Three hundred copies were made, each signed by the three authors. In September *Travels in Nihilon*, an inventive study of what could happen in a purely nihilistic state, was released. The response from critics and the public was muted, and the initial printing run has been enough to satisfy demand. In the meantime he was continuing to work steadily on a volume of literary autobiography entitled *Raw Material*. Alternating chapters were to be devoted to an examination of the nature of artistic creation and definitions of 'truth' in that context, and a dissection of Sillitoe's family background with particular emphasis on the dominating physical and spiritual presence of one man, his imperious grandfather Burton. Predictably, *Raw Material* received a lot of attention when it was published in 1972. The chance to watch any important writer dipping into the wellspring of his imagination to analyse his creative processes has always intrigued students of literature. In the case of Sillitoe, whose early work had clearly developed outside the conventional middle-class traditions of the English novel, the prospect provoked greater interest than usual. Though uneven in its execution, the book offers a number of insights not only into the kinds of things Sillitoe feels deeply about, but also into the ways in which his peculiar sensibility functions. Sillitoe himself sees *Raw Material* as one of his most important books, and was gratified when a new, slightly revised, edition was released in 1978.

Sillitoe's Nottinghamshire origins may have prompted an invitation from Stephen Spender later in 1972 to contribute to a symposium on D. H. Lawrence. The resultant paper, entitled 'Lawrence and District', was included in a collection of essays entitled *Mountains and Caverns* which Sillitoe published in 1975. Another kind of return to Nottingham took place with the release of the film version of *The Ragman's Daughter*. Directed by Harold Becker, it featured Victoria Tennant in the title role. Two actors were needed to play Tony Bradmore, the narrator of the original story: the teenage Tony was played by Simon Rouse, and Patrick

O'Connell played Tony as a man of thirty-five. Reviews were mixed, there was little promotion, and the film did not have a wide distribution. By now, after spending three years in the country, Sillitoe decided that Wittersham was not as convenient a place to live as he had originally hoped, and late in the year he returned with his family to London. Suitable accommodation was found in a flat in Notting Hill Gate, but the house in Wittersham was kept on for holiday use and as a retreat.

There was little time for travel abroad in 1973, though in April he gave a series of readings at the universities of Bordeaux and Nantes. In October he published a fresh collection of stories, *Men, Women and Children*. It was well received, in particular because of 'Mimic', the compelling and original story which began the collection. In the meantime Sillitoe was struggling with the manuscript of the final novel in his trilogy, begun eight years before with *The Death of William Posters* and followed in 1967 by *A Tree on Fire*. He had begun the new novel in 1967, but there was still nearly three-quarters of it to write, and it was uphill going. Partly because he had lost the impetus that writing the earlier works one after the other had provided, and partly because there seemed to be relatively little new for his protagonist to say, the novel resisted his attempts to shape it and give it point. The final draft was entitled *The Flame of Life* and published the following year. It is without doubt his weakest work.

In 1974 Sillitoe visited Israel and the United States, both for the first time. By now he had become strongly and vocally pro-Zionist in his views. In a letter to *The Times* the previous October, for example, he had argued for the continued Israeli occupation of Sinai, the Golan Heights and the east bank of the Jordan as 'the only guarantee of [Israel's] continued safety'. In May he was invited by the Israeli Foreign Office to spend ten days in the country to observe the land and its people at first hand. Though he made copious notes during the trip, he has so far kept his impressions to himself, though he did publish two short articles in a geographical journal shortly after he returned home. It was his interest in geography which led him to the United States later in the year. In October he responded to an invitation to give a series of lectures in the Department of Geography at Nebraska State University. One of these, entitled 'Maps', appeared in the *Geographical Magazine* and was later included in *Mountains and Caverns*.

In 1974 Sillitoe was also becoming more vocal in his criticism of repression inside the Soviet Union. In an article published in *The Times* and entitled 'When will the Russians see that humanity is good for them?' he argued passionately for the granting of exit visas to Soviet citizens who wanted to join relatives in the West, and in particular for two people whose circumstances he knew of personally. This sense of involvement with the suffering of others, always a hallmark of his fiction, was also evident in a collection of poems he published in 1974 entitled *Storm*. The new selection included the poems he had published jointly with Ruth Fainlight and Ted Hughes three years before, as well as a number of short lyrics which had appeared in small press editions entitled *Shaman* and *Barbarians* in 1968 and 1973. Taken together, they reveal a marked advance in Sillitoe's poetic technique and control of his subject matter. In this, and in their ability to evoke a powerful response from the reader, they deserve serious consideration.

During the next two years Sillitoe published little, though *Mountains and Caverns* appeared in November, 1975. It contained essays and speeches written since 1963, and included a previously unpublished recollection of his early years entitled 'The Long Peace'. He also continued to involve himself in humanitarian causes, writing regularly to *The Times* and taking part in conferences. He was present at a UNESCO-sponsored conference held in Brussels in March, 1975, which discussed Arab–Israeli confrontation over cultural activities, and the following year he attended a similar conference in Paris. In November he was gratified to learn of his election as a Fellow of the Royal Geographical Society. In February, 1976, he spoke to a conference on Soviet Jewry in Brussels, condemning Russian treatment of Jews who wanted to leave the country. And in the meantime, of course, he was writing. Work continued on a major new novel whose protagonist was a career army officer, and this necessitated many months of research at the Royal Military Academy at Woolwich. On September 16 a short play entitled *The Interview*, which he had been commissioned to write in aid of Soviet Jewry, was performed by Janet Suzman, Colin Blakeley and Jerry Sunquist at St Martins-in-the-Fields. A number of poems and short stories were also produced during this period, and revisions were made to the children's story, 'Big John and the Stars', in preparation for its publication as a book.

Much of this activity came to fruition late in 1976 and early the following year. *The Widower's Son*, Sillitoe's ninth novel, appeared in November. A clear departure from most of his earlier work, it offered an acute assessment of a master gunner bred from boyhood to army life and attitudes, both during and after his period of military service. It was highly praised on publication in England, and provoked an enthusiastic critical and popular reception on its release in the United States a few months later. *Big John and the Stars*, with illustrations by Agnes Molnar, was released by Robson Books early in the new year. Set in the Valley of Gold 'at a time when the world was young, in an age too far off for anyone to remember', it tells of Big John, 'a blacksmith with a fiery red beard', and how he came to make stars for the whole world. Like the best children's literature, the story manages to present great truths in a simple way, explaining things in a plausible yet magical manner which stimulates and liberates a child's imagination. It deserves to be widely read. In September 'Pit Strike', one of the short stories published in *Men, Women and Children*, was dramatised on BBC Television as part of a series designed to encourage the work of young directors. Roger Bumford, who directed the dramatisation, met the challenges of the story admirably, and chose well in casting Brewster Mason as the protagonist Joshua.

In the meantime Sillitoe had been invited by the mayor of Jerusalem to spend part of the summer with his family at the Mishkenot Sha' ananim, a retreat known as the 'dwellings of serenity' to which well-known artists and other creative people are often invited as guests of the city. Sillitoe had been fascinated by Israel since childhood, an enthusiasm he described in 'My Israel', an article for the 1974 Christmas issue of the *New Statesman*, and he readily accepted the invitation. As it turned out, he was there for the better part of two months, taking the opportunity to visit remote parts of the country, and keeping an account of his impressions in a daily journal. Since returning to England he has completed the draft of a new novel and spent much of the winter revising it. In March of 1978 his one-act play, *The Interview*, was performed at the Almost Free Theatre in London in an extended and revised version. Part of a series of plays about prejudice and its responses presented in association with the Ben Uri Theatre Group, it examines the problems of a Russian Jewess who is applying for an exit visa in order to live in Israel. Irina, the Jewess, was played by Diana Fairfax, her interrogator by Glyn Owen, and a fellow prisoner by John Rees. The play was directed by Jack Emery. In April the revised edition of *Raw Material* was released, and late in the same month Robson Books published a short children's story entitled *The Incredible Fencing Fleas*. A book of plays including *This Foreign Field* (retitled *The Slot Machine*), *The Interview* and *Pit Strike* and entitled *Three Plays*, was published in December 1978.

At the age of fifty, twenty years after the publication of *Saturday Night and Sunday Morning*, Alan Sillitoe is at the midpoint of his career. He has produced a considerable volume of work, and the fiction is all still in print and likely to remain so for the foreseeable future. His reputation is both enhanced and bedevilled by the talents he exhibited in describing working-class life so well in the early fiction. It is generally assumed today that he has no peer as an accurate and compassionate chronicler of working-class life, but only a careful assessment of his early work will put us in a position to judge the validity of such an assumption or, for that matter, to evaluate his more recent work. It may be that in the long run Sillitoe's early working-class fiction will be eclipsed by later, more mature, work. But that is a question for readers twenty or more years hence to answer, when there is likely to be a much larger body of work on which to make an assessment.

Notes and References

[1] Quotations in this chapter have been selected from Sillitoe's own essays and speeches, and occasionally from reviews or interviews in which he is quoted. Published material is listed in the bibliography.

[2] The fate of his own work at the hands of Soviet censors, which he was to learn of in detail some years later, is recounted in his introduction to a new edition of *Key to the Door* (W. H. Allen, 1978) and documented by Maurice Friedburg in *A Decade of Euphoria: Western Literature in Post-Stalin Russia, 1954–64* (Indiana University Press, 1977).

Chapter Three

Critical Perspectives:

Sillitoe's Views on Writing

Alan Sillitoe shares with Shelley the belief that the serious writer should be a solitary leader, 'beyond and outside the values of the age he lives in, like a watch hand set at twelve o'clock, with the rest of mankind in the middle of the dial and moving towards five-to-eleven.'[1] The stance is unoriginal, but it is Sillitoe's way of proclaiming an individual social commitment which on the one hand preserves 'the old, perhaps romantic, idea of the poet and novelist working alone in the darkness', and on the other affirms the view that 'the advance guard of art is the life spirit of society.' This strong sense of the writer's independent voice echoes and re-echoes throughout Sillitoe's critical statements, whether they are concerned with the creative imagination, with the novelist's aims and purpose, with technical problems of symbolic or thematic content, or with the work of other writers.

Sillitoe has consistently sought to weave a mystique about the creative processes of the novelist. His images of the artist range from the mythic to the mundane: 'writers are both victims and heroes of fate.' A writer of fiction is like 'Saint George fighting and vanquishing the dragon of language in order to marry the princess of art.' He works with words as a 'blacksmith uses the tools of his strong and often subtle art.' And he is 'like a coal miner ... in the dark, quarrying against narrow and difficult seams thousands of years old, coming now and again onto something that appears valuable and worth digging out.' The choice of metaphors is meant to reinforce an idea of the artist as an initiate of a mysteriously knowledgeable group, far removed from the normal life of the average reader.

Developing his image of the miner, Sillitoe says that 'a writer brings up what to him alone shines in the darkness. ... He uses senses that those who live on the surface don't always imagine existing.' However, Sillitoe fails to elaborate on or define these 'senses'. Instead he romanticises the creative process as an attempt

> to clarify the misty and occasionally musty vision of a face whose features are involved in some form of emotion, suffering in particular circumstances that force me to the act of recording them on the seismograph of my own mind. The face need not be one that is surfacing out of some far-off memory, may never have been seen or sensed but comes complete and strong out of the imagination ... from I don't know where, or even out of a dream, some twisted drama neither fact nor fiction but instead a forked memory that my mother and father once had but that I never did and that they never told me.

The passage evokes Jung's theory of a collective unconscious, with which the writer claims to be in touch. But Sillitoe confuses the issue by limiting the source of material to his own parents. The distinctly esoteric ring of the passage is echoed in his acceptance speech on winning the Hawthornden Award for *The Loneliness of the Long-Distance Runner*. In the speech he declared that

> the award, though made out in my name, is not given to me personally, but to ... the story, words that merely passed through my brain and hand and pen from some source over which I have little or no responsibility – but for which I have a great deal of respect. ... What I am

trying to say is that if a man writes a poem, he has no right to accept praise for the poem, though he may feel glad that he was chosen to write it. ... The same goes for anything else, stories, novels, paintings, symphonies. ... The writer may be in touch with imagination, but it doesn't belong to him.

Despite their apparent confusion, the two passages just quoted are particularly helpful to the reader who wishes to understand Sillitoe's work, for they do reveal him as a writer who expects to be taken seriously, who hopes that whatever message he conveys in his work will be received as authoritative. In effect his statements are special pleading for consideration of the writer as a kind of prophet, a man who has been 'chosen' to reveal truth to other men. In other words, they attempt to create an authority for the writer which will lend weight to whatever pronouncements on human affairs he makes in his work. (They may also indicate, of course, that in the early stages of his career, Sillitoe was not fully confident of his own talent, as the phrases 'force me to the act of recording' and 'some source over which I have little or no responsibility' suggest.) All this is particularly important to Sillitoe since he has consistently concerned himself with social doctrine, and with recording the problems he finds in contemporary society and pointing the way to their solution.

Sillitoe feels that every work of fiction should be an intensely idiosyncratic statement, the projection of an individual writer's unique views of man in society. But while the work should be anchored in reality so that it is easily recognised as a picture of the contemporary world, it may also have a mythic or a symbolic dimension. For Sillitoe this usually means that the work in question reveals archetypal yearnings or prejudices which have some continuing social relevance. His commentary on John Arden's play *Serjeant Musgrave's Dance*, for example, reflects this attitude: 'When Musgrave arrives at the colliery town with his patrol of deserters, his packing cases of gatling-gun and skeleton of their comrade killed in a futile colonial war, you have a situation that is mythic in its impact, making a play which would appeal to ... working-class audiences.' What Sillitoe is discussing here is an appeal to deep-rooted anti-authoritarianism which is also very much in evidence in his own early fiction.

Sillitoe also believes that for socially relevant literature to be effective 'the symbolism must merge with the realism.' This view is conventional enough and somewhat vague as well, though Sillitoe has attempted to illustrate his meaning from his own work. In his third novel, *Key to the Door*, the hero and some companions decide to scale a Malayan mountain they can see from their air force barracks. The physical difficulties of the attempt are carefully described, and the evolving attitudes of some of the participants are recorded in detail. In an interview about the novel for *Books and Bookmen* Sillitoe said that he 'meant the mountain-climb to represent useless striving, [and] the emptiness in ideas like patriotism;' illustrating how a realistically described incident might contain a symbolic dimension as well. From such remarks on Arden's work and his own it is evident that for Sillitoe symbolic levels of meaning are unimportant in themselves, and should function ideally only in combination with the realistic elements of a story to reinforce the social message being presented.

The serious writer today has a two-fold duty, according to Sillitoe. First he should concern himself with themes which reflect contemporary social injustice, and second he should continually remind his readers of the need for reform. Too few writers, he said in one article, follow this independent course. Most are content 'to support the societies whose air they breath [sic] and whose bread they eat' and to reproduce familiar patterns of socially acceptable ideas which make no demands on the reader. He speaks of having found it difficult himself 'to learn to write, to break through barriers of cliché and influence before being able to draw from what exists behind my own voice.' And in judging a fiction contest sponsored by *sixth form opinion* he urged the aspiring young writers to adopt a similarly independent course. He praised the lack of apparent literary influences in their work 'because it proves that the story and theme dominated the writer, rather than anything else she or he had read before;' and he went on to tell them that good writers 'ignore critics, publishers, friends, editors and immerse themselves in their work.' It should be pointed out, however, that in an un-published manuscript entitled 'Chance Reading' and in other articles Sillitoe contradicts the implication here that all literary influence should be avoided, by talking at some length about the works that influenced him.

Elsewhere he suggests that the aspiring writer should fight against becoming 'the shallow man who speaks clichés in a situation presented a thousand times before ... which tell us nothing.' He must strive, instead, says Sillitoe, to become a 'good writer', that is, one who is 'saying "yes" to life, even though the "yes" may be hidden in complexities or experi-mentation, or criticism.' Ironically Sillitoe's advice here takes the form of a cliché, and the reader is at a loss to extract a precise meaning from it. In the context of other comments he has made, though, it would seem that Sillitoe is saying that serious writers should share his particular social con-victions if they expect to produce worthwhile literature. This rather prejudiced view is echoed in a *TLS* article entitled 'Both Sides of the Street', in which Sillitoe argues that there are basically two kinds of writers – the man of the Right and the man of the Left. The former is content to accept and repeat the values and attitudes of the society he lives in. The latter is a 'truly creative writer ... a revolutionary', whose nature rebels against accepting easy social clichés and con-ventionalities. On the one hand are those 'lauded and popular authors ... whose writing extols the society they live in, or accept it without any criticism.' On the other is the 'artist and rebel' whose revolt is 'a necessary breakwater against the evil of mindlessness ... into which the population seems somehow too ready and willing to be pushed.'

The pervasiveness of this simplistic outlook in Sillitoe's thoughts about literature (at least in the early stages of his career) is illustrated in his published critical comments on the work of other novelists in which, as late as 1965, he continually championed the cause of writers of the Left. He uses a review of J. B. Priestley's *Literature and Western Man*, for example, to inveigh against 'the false class-portrayal of Noel Coward and his myth of This Happy Breed.' And in a letter to *Books and Bookmen* he castigates novelists who still offer 'stiff-upper-lip sagas that uphold Kiplingesque imperial virtues as though they weren't by now anachronisms.' But he praises Conrad's *Nostromo* as 'a tale of cancer that lies at the core of imperialist exploitation no matter what its method.' Sillitoe has also used the reviewing stand to express a number of his characteristic opinions about society's ills. He begins a review of Edna Nixon's *Voltaire and the Calas Case* by quoting King Alfred's dictum that power is never good, except he be good that has it. He goes on to suggest that even 'when the good have power ... they soon learn to use it against those unfortunates who are born with the possibility of dislodging them from their position. Nonconformists, revolutionaries, deviationists – they are all considered evil because their views threaten the existing power.' This working-class anti-authoritarian bias is also evident in Sillitoe's condemnation of police brutality in a brief review of *Gangrene*, 'this anthology of modern oppression' edited by Peter Benenson. It shows up again in his comments on Sven Hassel's *The Wheels of Terror:* 'The statement here is that anyone who joins up is a potential war criminal. War is rotten. Conscription is immoral and illegal, no matter what laws are passed in favour of it. No country can call itself a democracy that keeps it on in peacetime. Conscription is the modern form of the press-gang, and the pity is that not enough young men are encouraged to get out of it.' In 'Chance Reading', commenting on *The Good Soldier Schweik*, he expresses a similar point of view: 'In Jaroslav Hasek's classic I saw how good-natured stupidity could be turned to a vitriolic rebellion against the forces of oppression. Who could join the army after reading about Schweik's adventures, and the author's wise and human comments upon them?' And in an article which examines a number of recent proletarian novels he singles out the work of John Petty for praise because the writer is 'an out and out uncompromiser with Government, who sees law-and-order as a menace to free men, a boon only to slaves and masters.' Literary merit for Sillitoe, at least in the first decade of his career, was affected to a great extent by the subject matter a given writer might choose as well as by his degree of commitment to social change. And his selection of essays for inclusion in *Mountains and Caverns* suggests that he still subscribed substantially to these criteria as late as 1975.

Sillitoe's preoccupation with the writer's role as independent social critic has also coloured his extended commentaries on other novelists. His interest in the work of Arnold Bennett, for example, stems partly from his experience of a similar Midlands provincial background and partly from what he considers Bennett's realistic representation of the social conditions of his time and place. Sillitoe believes that a writer's response to a particular kind of landscape can strongly influence his way of looking at life, and he vividly describes some peculiar features of the Midlands which can etch themselves on the writer's subconscious: 'the factory chimneys, the coombes and crags, the Severn at Ironbridge seen from afar like a silvery anaconda smashed to death among wooded Shropshire hills, the vast secret manufacturies among black valleys, diseased kilns and disused ginpits, forges and foundries, tips and slag heaps and smelting works, churned earth making the aftermath of Somme battles look like landscape for a Surrey cricket match.' He feels that the writer brought up on such uncompromising scenery is conditioned to viewing the world unsentimentally; he is able to see its difficulties and unpleasantness clearly. Such a man, forced to leave his home because of some inner need for other experience and perspective, can never escape the environmentally-conditioned way he has learned to observe life, and will continue to reflect this outlook in his work.

Sillitoe feels that Bennett's conditioning also allowed him

'to portray ordinary people in realistic terms and not as caricatures' and to draw his characters honestly and without sentimentality: 'Constance, Samuel Povey the draper's assistant, Maggie the servant, Gerald Scales, Sophia, Mrs Baines – none have that Dickensian sickliness that often pervaded the words of H. G. Wells.' Instead Sillitoe finds them to be socially exact representations of the English lower middle class, true to their time and place, and he commends Bennett for this social realism. Yet Sillitoe's critical myopia makes him take occasional exception to Bennett's work. He disagrees, for example, with Bennett's comments on the 'outrages of the workers during the Reform Riots of 1832 [which Sillitoe feels was] a mass uprising of people who, after all, wanted only a rough form of human rights.' And Sillitoe's strong belief in the role of the artist as crusader for social reform would not let him see greatness in a writer who 'states the tragedy, tells the story, and does not search for answers.' So although he finds Bennett one of the most faithful realists in English fiction, he does not consider him to be a great writer. Instead he sees him as one of the best regional novelists that England has produced, and sets him alongside the Eliot of *Middlemarch* and *Adam Bede* and the Hardy of *The Mayor of Casterbridge*. It must be added, however, that Sillitoe's own recent work, in which the 'search for answers' is much less obvious than in his earlier fiction, suggests that in a fresh appraisal of Bennett he would be inclined to see him in a more sympathetic light.

It is Sillitoe's contention that 'no society ... can be worthy of the name until it is able to tolerate those artists who do not support it.' He emphasises that the writer who goes his own way must not only be tolerated but encouraged: 'In the mass-communications age of today some writers find themselves intellectually committed to the society they live in, but those who cannot make such direct commitment are' an asset even if they criticise, for their 'art which is alive and in conflict with the world around [them] gives psychic energy to those who read it, disrupts and deepens the staid mind.' In this way Sillitoe sees the true artist as a kind of revolutionary, releasing through his provocative art an energy with the potential to revitalise society.

While Sillitoe has not defined the nature of this psychic energy precisely, it would seem that only novels which fulfill two of his criteria for good fiction – the recording of social ills and a call for reform – can have it. One such novel for him is Robert Tressell's *The Ragged Trousered Philanthropists*, first published in 1914 and released in a new edition with an introduction by Sillitoe in 1965. The novel recounts the problems of a group of builder's labourers and the attempts of one of their number, a decorator named Owen, to give them a belief in their own dignity and in their capacity for alleviating the misery of their lives. His efforts prove fruitless against the apathy of the workers, and he begins to call them philanthropists, giving their lives for the comfort of their 'betters'. Sillitoe sees the book both as an accurate historical record and as a call to action and social reform. He suggests that Tressell is describing faithfully 'the working people of his time [who] did not have the same clarity, violent outlook, nor intellectual guidance of those earlier men of the Industrial Revolution. Never before or since were they so spiritless or depressed.' The novel has continuing relevance for today's readers, Sillitoe affirms, especially for 'those whose life [sic] has touched the misery recounted by Robert Tressell [for they] can get out of it many things: a bolstering of class feeling; pure rage; reinforcement for their own self-pity; a call to action; maybe a good and beneficial dose of all these things.'

Sillitoe's statement that the best perspective for the writer on social reform is a working-class one was echoed in his approach to the socially committed writing of George Orwell. In an interview for *Reynolds News* he praised the authentic re-creation of working-class misery during the thirties in *The Road to Wigan Pier*, in which Orwell 'describes as an outsider what I was living at the age of eleven'; elsewhere he marvels at the 'painstaking and tortuous [sic] effort [in Orwell's writing which] made up for missing spontaneity, with the result that he never wrote a dull page.' This unqualified admiration for Orwell's prose is obviously coloured by Sillitoe's own strong feelings about the working-class; he is temperamentally in tune with a writer whose work chronicles social inequity and injustice and who calls for reform. While he suggests that Orwell's three English novels are a little too grim for reality and that he ignores even the occasional joys of people in difficult economic circumstances, Sillitoe does find 'one flicker of brightness' in *A Clergyman's Daughter* in the girl's realisation of a need for social action, 'working within the framework of her life to try and help other people.' It is no surprise that he finds *Homage to Catalonia* Orwell's least depressing work, since there 'he is actually participating in the class war with rifle and bayonet.' In the final analysis, Orwell's integrity as a writer who crusaded for social reform makes him for Sillitoe 'the best English writer by far to come out of the thirties.' And he finds Orwell's work still relevant because 'the slums and dilapidated slave-barracks described by him ... are still standing, only now there is a TV set in each one and food (of a sort) on every table.'

Sillitoe sees the writer as the champion of individualism pitted against governmental attempts at thought control. He feels that television, radio and the popular press have become mouthpieces of government or Establishment ideology, and that the writer of the Left must counter spreading apathy and comfortable addiction to old values. He must remain a rebel, hoping to overthrow the forces which promote mindlessness, and remain 'at the very least a threat to the monolithic other side.' To effect this, Sillitoe suggests that

> a writer should communicate in realities – by words that erode the symbols transmitted by government or advertising agencies. ... [People] are being neutralised by the message of good living, on the supposition that they will stay content as long as enough earthly bread is being given out.
>
> A writer must assume that people deserve something more than the cunning image of earthly bread. They

need ... a literature that will not only allow them to
see themselves as they are but one which will give them
the feeling of individual dignity that mass communica-
tion, by its own definition, is unable to transmit.

Sillitoe's idea of the writer as social revolutionary, suggesting
radical alteration in the class structure to eliminate inequities
and injustices, would at first seem to be Marxist in origin.
It should be pointed out, however, that he is unwilling to
commit himself to any precise doctrine for utopia, Marxist
or otherwise. And in his *TLS* article he specifically condemns
Marxism because 'both Marxists and advertisers have this
much in common: to them the ordinary people are "the
masses" and not individuals.'

Sillitoe's distrust of government and his rejection of the
authoritarianism and ultra-patriotic attitudes he associates
with it are reflected in his assertion that 'writers cannot begin
their warnings too early: they cannot too clearly spread distrust of authority and over-government.' He also suggests
that novelists who come from and write about the working-
class, are likely to make effective literary rebels, for they have
trained themselves to become writers under difficult circumstances in a section of society that gives little encouragement
to literary aspirations. The rebellious mentality needed for
this achievement reflects 'an individuality that can play its
part in opposing the mindlessness of this technological age,
encouraging ordinary people to think of themselves not as
a mass but as individuals, and ridding them of narrow patriotic attitudes, or [other] out-dated ideas.' The fiction that
these men produce, he says, should allow us to make better
use of the technological advances of our time by persuading
people 'to build ... [and] improve the world they live in.'
To date few working-class novelists have appeared to justify
or refute this supposition, though it would seem to be at the
very least a debatable thesis.

Sillitoe's fear of the possible misuses of modern advances
in communications is equalled by his zeal in crusading against
ideas he feels are outmoded. The idea of God, for example,

is called 'man's fatal neurosis' in the *TLS* essay, and war is 'one sort of psycho-analysis [that] has certainly failed to cure him of it.' He goes on to say that 'as soon as God is disregarded, and [the] human contest becomes one of man against nature, then the battles between men will cease, and be replaced by the simple problem of getting enough food and shelter for everybody.' In *Road to Volgograd* Sillitoe described himself as an atheist, though the assertion needs qualification, for in the *TLS* essay he is careful to define the God he rejects: 'As a child I was mind-manipulated by the society I grew up in, was brain-washed on going to school to think God good, my country right or wrong, cut-throat private business the only way to run a nation's economy, and war the best method of uniting a nation to defend its markets. These values were God.' He then singles out patriotism for particular denunciation, calling it 'that surviving evil of Athenian orators ... being converted these days for use against an ideology instead of a kink in some national boundary.' (Much later, in 1972, he expressed a continuing distaste for the manipulators of bellicose nationalism in a speech criticising the concept of the Olympic Games; it was later included in *Mountains and Caverns* under the title 'Sport and Nationalism'.) To counteract this practice he calls for 'new values of liberation ... a spiritual opening of both ideological and national boundaries under a universal government of technology set to contend with nature.' It is the duty of every artist, he asserts, to help bring this change about.

Vague and oversimplified though some of the statements just quoted are, they do provide additional evidence that Sillitoe's interest in literature is closely coupled with a commitment to dramatic social change. While he was still working on *The Death of William Posters*, Sillitoe commented on the relationship: 'Something new [in themes] has got to come. I'm not sure what it's going to be, but it's got to be something powerful and immediate to everyone. Something that everyone can identify with and feel passionately about. I keep asking myself what; but I haven't come up with a satisfactory answer yet. I've simply formulated three words for myself which are aimed in the direction I want to go. The words are PATIENCE, SUBVERSION, and ART.' The three words chosen to characterise his position succinctly restate Sillitoe's view of the artist as solitary, prizing his individual integrity while affirming his social commitment. On the one hand he recognises the need for patience in the painstaking production of good art, on the other he sees that patience is also necessary to plan and carry out effective subversion of what he considers an unjust social order.

In his critical commentaries Sillitoe frequently points out that the independent writer's duty is to convince his readers that dramatic social change is both necessary and inevitable. The methods he uses to achieve this end are perhaps less important to Sillitoe than the attempt itself. What matters is that his voice is being heard, committed and personal, offering passion and defiance to illuminate the social injustice he sees and to advocate progress and reform. Sillitoe's own fiction, most obviously in the Seaton saga and the first two novels of the trilogy, offers the reader a series of intriguing examples of his revolutionary critical credo put into practice. More recent work, though more subtle and controlled in some ways, continues to reveal his social concern by documenting the suffering of particular individuals at the hands of a society he clearly feels is still in need of thorough reappraisal.

Notes and References

[1] Quotations in this chapter have been selected from Sillitoe's essays and speeches, including reviews, introductions and critical articles on the nature of writing, written between 1958 and 1965. Published material is listed in the bibliography.

Chapter Four

A Sense of Identity:
Physical Conditions of
Working-class Life

One of the prominent characteristics of the English novel since its inception has been a concern with class. Ian P. Watt points out in *The Rise of the Novel* that middle-class habits and attitudes in the eighteenth century gave the new genre its impetus and a large measure of its subject matter as well. Serious nineteenth century novels were often concerned with problems of social mobility, and according to Louis James in *Fiction for the Working Man 1830–1850* a great deal of journalistic fiction was written specifically for working-class readers. In the twentieth century the importance of class continues to be recognised and used by contemporary novelists. As James Gindin records in *Postwar British Fiction: New Accents and Attitudes*, 'in an age without world-wide political or metaphysical assurances, the intellectual frequently... talks of the specific social problem because he can make more sense out of it than he can out of the problems of nuclear warfare or the existence of God. Class, for the contemporary intellectual, often serves as a limited and sensible substitute for far greater and more overwhelming issues, a limited topic through which he can express some perception and some control.'

This artistic concern with class mirrors an important part of a larger national consciousness. For centuries Englishmen have been particularly aware of hierarchical patterns in their society, and the careful structuring of classes has even been attributed at times to divine ordination, as William Hewlett's well-known hymn illustrates:

> The rich man at his castle,
> The poor man at his gate,
> He made them high and lowly
> And ordered their estate.
> All things bright and beautiful.

Definition of these classes has naturally varied a good deal with time and individual commentators, and until the eighteen-seventies at least, according to Henry Pelling in *A Short History of the Labour Party*, it was 'usual to speak of "the labouring classes" or "the middle classes" in the plural, thus recognising the variety to be found under both descriptions.' Twentieth century writers, however, have usually favoured the terms 'working-class', 'middle-class' and 'aristocracy', though variants are still common. While it is evident that since the Second World War even the lines between these categorisations have become blurred, G. D. H. Cole still held in *The Post-War Condition of Britain* in 1956 that 'class distinctions, though they are often said to be breaking down, preserve a considerable vitality in most people's minds.' Three years later Richard Hoggart, in his perceptive analysis of working-class life entitled *The Uses of Literacy*, pointed out that while it is frequently assumed 'that already most of us inhabit an almost flat plain of the lower middle-to-middle classes', yet there is a world of the working-class still flourishing. In his book Hoggart focused on a sample homogenous group of working-class people in an attempt to 'evoke the atmosphere, the quality of their lives by describing their setting and their attitudes.' A number of post-war novelists have also felt that a comprehensive description of social and class background is necessary to an understanding of man's actions in the modern world. Gindin acknowledged this formative importance of environment when he pointed out that 'because, in contemporary fiction and drama, men are to a great extent products of the time and place in which they were born and educated, writers spend a good deal of time outlining, describing, and accounting for time and place.' Consequently, since Alan Sillitoe is one of those whose early work follows this pattern, it is particularly important to isolate and define significant aspects of the physical working-class milieu he describes in the Nottingham fiction.

According to Cole, even for Englishmen class is a 'term of singularly elusive meaning. When it is used in ordinary conversation, one has usually a fairly clear notion of what is meant. But it remains very difficult to offer any precise definition.' Nonetheless, it is necessary to provide some general frame of reference for the specific study of Sillitoe's fictional representation of working-class life. It should be pointed out, however, that the general description of such life given here is based mainly on studies published during the nineteen-fifties and may vary in degree from conditions found in more recent years. A description of people normally thought of as belonging to the working-class might sensibly begin, then, with an occupational reference. A large percentage of them are unskilled or semi-skilled manual workers, often employed at routine jobs in a factory, large firm or shop. Some may be self-employed, running small retail shops to serve the needs of the area in which they live, or perhaps offering a service such as cutting hair or repairing shoes, furniture or bicycles. Generally they work for a weekly wage, with income limited to this single source, sometimes without sick-time benefit. Many children take advantage of the official school-leaving age at fifteen to begin their working lives early. As a result, their wages are more or less permanently fixed in relation to the cost of living, and they have relatively little job security. Though estimates vary widely, a figure of twelve pounds per week may be taken as a reasonable average for the head of a family in the mid-fifties, and this represents roughly a fifty per cent rise over pre-war incomes. The majority of working-class families live in cities, in their own recognisable areas usually distinguished by rows of ageing back-to-back houses with two rooms upstairs and two down. Their lives have traditionally been centred on a limited local district, with its own shops and pubs providing a self-contained circle of involvement. Finally, it should be remembered that this sense of community is reinforced by the sharing of a large number of attitudes on a wide variety of topics, characterised generally by a strong sense of class solidarity pitting *us* against the outside world of *them*.

Alan Sillitoe's own background is used to advantage in his early fiction. In setting his early work mainly in and around post-war Nottingham, Sillitoe uses familiar locale, peculiar urban sights, sounds and smells along with patterns of activity in factories, homes and streets to create a fictional working-class world that is firmly anchored in recognisable reality. A strong sense of place pervades nearly all Sillitoe's fiction. More than a hundred names of Nottingham city streets and nearby areas in the countryside echo and re-echo in the early novels, *Saturday Night and Sunday Morning* and *Key to the Door*, and in the short stories published in *The Loneliness of the Long-Distance Runner* and *The Ragman's Daughter*. The reader soon becomes familiar with urban landmarks like 'Slab' Square, Canning Circus and Nottingham Castle, the rivers Trent and Leen and the bridges that span them, main arteries like Castle Boulevard and the Mansfield, Hartley, Alfreton, Ilkeston and Derby Roads, streets of back-to-backs in Radford and working-class neighbourhoods known locally as The Meadows and Sodom. Alfreton Road, for instance, is a typical part of this world, 'wide and cobbled, bordered by scrapyards, toyshops, pubs, pawnbrokers, cheap grocery stores, the livewire artery for back-to-backs and factories hanging like clogs on either side. People carried bundles to the pawnshop or sackbags to the scrapyard, or came up from town with untouched dole or wages in their pockets so that trading went on every day of the week' (Key: 166)[1]. This urban setting is bounded by the nearby partially built-up areas of Strelley and Trowel, Lenton and Wollaton, Eastwood and the Bramcote Hills, and it is normally within these circumscribed limits that Sillitoe's characters act out the dramas of their lives.

Members of the Seaton family, who dominate *Saturday Night and Sunday Morning* and *Key to the Door*, are particularly attuned to the rhythms of urban life. Harold Seaton, the principal breadwinner of the family, 'clung to the town centre because its burrow was familiar and comfortable' while his wife Vera, a first generation city dweller, 'missed the sound of factory engines and traffic' on a visit to her parents in the country (Key: 17, 44). Their son Brian, the hero of *Key to the Door*, reacts in a similar way. In the heat of a Malayan jungle he is nostalgic about the city: 'I wish I was in Nottingham out of this blood-sucking sun, back where it's cool and my brain will clear so's I can start to think' (Key: 353). On leave from the Air Force later he feels 'the excitement in him ... at the sensation in his stomach of being lost once more in the vast familiar spider's web of Nottingham and all the comfortable meaning of it' (Key: 388). His brother Arthur, hero of *Saturday Night and Sunday Morning*, and their elder brother Fred found on going home after an evening's pub crawl that 'the maze of streets sleeping between tobacco factory and bicycle factory drew them into the enormous spread of its suburban bosom and embraced them in sympathetic darkness' (SNSM: 113).

For Sillitoe's characters, streets are usually more inviting than fields and open country. Dave Doddoe, a cousin of the Seaton brothers, finds 'the soaked smell of the green and soily earth' in the countryside beyond Ambergate 'extreme and frightening' and he comments: 'They have wicked weather out here. ... Only a month ago the snow nearly covered the telephone poles. I'd rather be in streets' (RD: 132, 135). Brian Seaton thinks of 'the desolation of stark countryside. ... If not snow, then the fields were dull and wet under a grey sky, and there was no comfort in crossing fields and mud like a fugitive walking beyond the world of sound. ... Streets were better' (Key: 158). And Arthur is aware in winter how 'each dark street patted his shoulder and became a friend. ... Houses lay in rows and ranks, a measure of safety in such numbers, and those within were snug and grateful fugitives from the broad track of bleak winds that brought rain from the Derbyshire mountains and snow from the Lincolnshire Wolds' (SNSM: 162). This architectural rhetoric, in which patterns of streets and houses are frequent points of reference, helps to mark the characters in Sillitoe's early work as urban men. While some of them do experience occasional nostalgia for a rural past, and find temporary respite from routine patterns of urban life in brief excursions to the country, their sense of identity is clearly defined by the city environment they normally inhabit. At the same time they recognise that the physical circumstances of life in working-class neighbourhoods are by no means paradisal. Streets can also be 'black and smothercating', the atmosphere surrounding back-to-back terraces can be permeated by 'disinfectant-suds, grease and newly-cut steel' from nearby factories and backyards.

Two recurrent physical factors that seem to characterise Sillitoe's working-class world best in the early fiction are noise and a lack of individual privacy. The Seaton family, for example, rarely escape industrial noises, even though they change houses a number of times. Their various places of residence include at least half a dozen identifiable Nottingham locations in Peters Street, Mount Street, Wilford Road, Albion Yard, and near the Faraday Road railway tracks, yet they are usually within earshot of factories which produce articles ranging from bicycles and guns to cardboard, stockings, hairnets and lace. Their situation in The Meadows, a euphemistically named 'aging suburb of black houses and small factories', is typical (LLDR: 133). Though sounds are somewhat muted inside their house near the bicycle works, 'once out of doors they were more aware of the factory rumbling a hundred yards away over the high wall. Generators whined all night, and during the day giant milling-machines working away on cranks and pedals in the turnery gave to the terrace a sensation of living within breathing distance of some monstrous being that suffered from a disease of the stomach' (SNSM: 25). Other families are even less fortunate, as the narrator of 'The Disgrace of Jim Scarfedale' recalls: 'Jim Scarfedale lived in our terrace, with his mam, in a house like our own, only it was a lot nearer the bike factory....

[while visiting them] I could hear the engines and pulleys next door in the factory thumping away, and iron-presses slamming as if they were trying to burst through the wall and set up another department at the Scarfedales' (LLDR: 140). As might be expected, the racket within the factory walls is equally disconcerting. When Arthur Seaton arrived at his job at the bicycle works on Monday morning, for example, he found the 'ring of the clocking-in machine made a jarring note', and once inside he 'allowed himself to be swallowed by its diverse noises, walked along lanes of capstan lathes and millers, drills and polishers and hand-presses, worked by a multiplicity of belts and pulleys turning and twisting and slapping. . . . Machines with their own small motors started with a jerk and a whine ... increasing a noise that made the brain reel and ache' (SNSM: 28).

Despite their exposure to the din of the factories, however, Sillitoe's workers frequently immerse themselves in other kinds of noisy communal activity. At Goose Fair, the Nottingham carnival held each autumn, Arthur Seaton along with his mistress and her sister enjoy listening to 'the thumping pistons of red-painted engines that gave power to Caterpillars and Noah's Arks, and distant screams [which] came down at them from the tower of Helter Skelter and the topmost arc of the Big Wheel, noise and lights a magnetised swamp sucking people into it for miles around' (SNSM: 156). And the record of Arthur's escapades in *Saturday Night and Sunday Morning* begins with his involvement in a crowded pub with a 'rowdy gang of singers' clamorously celebrating a victory by the local football team (SNSM: 7). His parents follow a similar noisy pattern, singing and drinking at a pub called the Marquis of Lorne on weekend nights. And Brian Seaton recalls that the entire family celebrated victory in 1945 at the pub, singing out their 'happiness in the biggest booze-up anybody could remember' (Key: 369).

It is clear throughout the early fiction that the continual aural bombardment from external sources provokes a response in kind from Sillitoe's working-class characters. Their relationships are usually characterised by direct and immediate expression of feelings, untempered by either tact or circumlocution. Even family quarrels are intensely vocal, and verbal disputes are often accompanied by physical violence. A number of stories in *The Loneliness of the Long-Distance Runner* illustrate this tendency. In 'On Saturday Afternoon' the narrator recalls how his father's black looks over the lack of a packet of cigarettes could quickly flare up into a verbal quarrel 'and before you know what's happening he's tipped up a tableful of pots and mam's gone out of the house crying. Dad hunches back over the fire and goes on swearing' (LLDR : 118–19). A domestic battle in 'The Match' reaches its climax when the husband 'picked up the plate of fish and, with exaggerated deliberation, threw it on the floor. "There," he roared. "That's what you do with your bleeding tea." "You're a lunatic," she screamed. "You're mental." He hit her once, twice, three times across the head, and knocked her to the ground. The little boy wailed, and his sister came running in from the parlour' (LLDR : 137). And Harry's wife in 'The Fishing Boat Picture' objects violently to his attempted escape from his physical environment through reading: '"You booky bastard," she screamed, "nowt but books, books, books, you bleddy dead-'ead"' whereupon she throws his books into the open fireplace (LLDR : 82).

Tensions fostered by crowded living accommodation may account in part for this volatile nature in Sillitoe's characters. Aunt Ada's household, for example, is in a state of continual pandemonium, frequently packed with her eleven children by Doddoe, her first husband, and the five others she is bringing up for Ralph, her second mate. In such close quarters friction is inevitable and battles are common, but the expression of a desire for personal privacy is rare. In all the early fiction only three characters could fairly be called 'readers' – Harry in 'The Fishing Boat Picture', Jim Scarfedale's wife in 'The Disgrace of Jim Scarfedale', and Brian Seaton in *Key to the Door* – and in each case their activity is regarded as abnormal by other members of the family. The verbal and physical violence bred by enforced proximity is accepted by most of Sillitoe's working-class people as an inevitable part of family life.

Their conditioning to this state of gregarious existence begins early, and siblings refer to one another as 'our Alma' or 'our Dave'. As a child Arthur Seaton has to share a bed with his two brothers, Brian and Fred, and though he later tells his girlfriend Doreen that 'being alone is a treat' because he comes from a large family and works in a crowded factory, he nevertheless usually seeks out companionship for his leisure activities (SNSM: 145). He finds no pleasure in going to a pub alone, for example, for 'in a half-filled pub he felt strangely isolated from the rest of his familiar world. . . . To be alone seemed a continuation of his drugged life at the lathe. He wanted noise, to drink and make love' (SNSM: 166).

The irritations of enforced togetherness are sometimes amusing to the reader. The amorous mood of Arthur's courtship, for instance, is thoroughly frustrated by the presence of a third person in the family living room: ' "Your mother teks all night to read that newspaper," he remarked. . . . "She reads every word of it," Doreen replied. "She loves the newspaper, more than a book" ' (SNSM: 205). But the difficulty of securing or being able to afford independent accommodation forces Arthur and Doreen to plan to live with her mother after marriage 'paying half the rent' (SNSM: 212). Similarly, Brian and his wife Pauline move in with her parents: 'Their names were down on the council housing list, but nothing would be ready, they realised, until years after he'd come out of the air force' (Key: 398).

The milieu of post-war municipal council housing projects known as 'estates' remains outside Sillitoe's portrayal of working-class life. His characters continue to inhabit the more primitive, ageing, back-to-backs near the factories, where their living conditions are essentially the same as they were before the war, apart from the appearance of more material goods such as television sets and washing machines. The houses are old, dirty and often bug-ridden. Brian Seaton remembers living before the war with his family in 'the bug-eaten back-to-backs of Albion Yard' and how 'in every staging-post of a house they found bugs, tiny oxblood buttons that hid within the interstices of bed-ticks, or secreted themselves below the saddles of their toes. Cockroaches also fought . . . over the kitchen floor' (Key: 9, 17). And his brother Arthur notices the age and dirt of their post-war house: 'red-ochre had been blackened by soot, paint was faded and cracked, everything was a hundred years old except the funiture inside' (SNSM: 26). Other primitive conditions include lack of bath facilities – in *Saturday Night and Sunday Morning* a zinc tub is brought into the kitchen for Brenda's hot-bath-with-gin abortion attempt – and outside lavatories.

The houses themselves are small inside, having a kitchen and living-room (occasionally called a parlour) on the main floor, and two bedrooms upstairs, and they are usually crowded with the paraphernalia of daily existence. Standing in the living-room belonging to Brenda, his married mistress, Arthur Seaton smells 'faint odours of rubber and oil coming from [her husband] Jack's bicycle leaning against a dresser that took up nearly one whole side of the room. . . . [and observes] old-fashioned chairs and a settee, fireplace, clock ticking on the mantelpiece, a smell of brown paper, soil from a plant-pot . . . and mustiness of rugs laid down under the table and by the fireplace' (SNSM: 16). Later in the novel he goes home with Doreen to find 'a kitchen smelling of stale gas and washed clothes. The living-room was untidy. . . . A line of dry washing hung diagonally across the room, and both dresser and shelf were crowded with old recumbent Christmas cards, snapshots standing against hairbrushes, clocks with no hands, and cigarette packets [as well as] a twenty-year-old wireless crackling from the dresser' (SNSM: 204). Yet it is in rooms like these, crowded with things as well as people, that one begins to discover a basis for the strong feelings of class identification and solidarity that Sillitoe attributes to his working-class characters. For just as Arthur Seaton finds 'a measure of safety' in the numerous rows and ranks of urban houses against the elemental harshness of nature, so these rooms provide others with a sense of homeliness and security that defies the machinations of an unpredictable and uncontrollable outside world. As Nan, the housewife in 'The Magic Box', puts it: ' "As long as you've got a pleasant place to live in there ain't much as can happen to you" ' (RD: 96). Her husband Fred quickly agrees. And when Arthur Seaton relaxes at home, he is able to reflect that 'it was a good, comfortable life if you didn't weaken, safe from the freezing world in a warm, snug kitchen, watching the pink and prominent houses of the opposite terrace' (SNSM: 46).

These instances of emotional reaction and clichéd expression, point to other distinguishing features of working-class life in Sillitoe's Nottingham fiction. The thoughts of his characters, for example, normally grow out of and are frequently limited to the immediate economic environment. (One example of this lack of imaginative stimulus is evident in the repetitive use of Christian names in the early fiction. There are, for instance, no less than five Teds, three Freds, three Bernards, three characters called Ernest or Ernie, three Almas, three girls named Doris as well as Dora, Doreen and Pauline, Arthur Seaton's relatives Bert and Albert, two Alfreds, two Mikes and two Harrys, two Joans, a Jane and a June.) Before the war most working-class boys such as Brian Seaton and the narrator in 'The Firebug' went to work at the age of fourteen. Later, when the official school leaving age was raised to fifteen, the drawing power of a wage packet remained stronger for many than any attractions continued studies might offer. The point is underlined by the difficulties experienced by Mr Raynor the school-teacher (in the story of the same name) handling an unruly 'C stream of fourteen-year-old louts raring [sic] to leave and start work at the factories round about' (LLDR: 71). And for some, such as the narrator in 'The Disgrace of Jim Scarfedale', beginning work is considered a coming of age: 'I'll never let anybody try and tell me that you don't have to sling your hook as soon as you get to the age of fifteen. You ought to be able to do it earlier, only it's against the law' (LLDR: 139). Predictably, however, most of Sillitoe's young workers soon find that their low level of education places severe restrictions on the kinds of jobs they can get and the amount of wages they can expect to earn from them.

Sillitoe says in the autobiographical short story 'The Decline and Fall of Frankie Buller' that 'the outspoken ambition of our class was to become one's own boss', but few of his characters are able to make the dream a reality (LLDR : 173). Those who do manage to run a small shop or service business usually find their financial independence limited and precarious. Instead, factories dominate the working lives of most characters in the Nottingham fiction. Nearly two-thirds of the men and an even higher percentage of the women, who work for a few years before marrying at nineteen or twenty, hold jobs in local factories. Sons frequently take jobs similar to those held by their fathers and sometimes even work for the same firm. Arthur Seaton and his father Harold, for example, are both employed in the bicycle plant where Arthur is at first a messenger boy and later a capstan lathe operator and his father holds a viewer's job checking parts in the three-speed shop. Young men usually begin as general labourers, and can consider themselves lucky if they are given light work such as the sweeping job held by Colin, the narrator in 'The Bike'. Brian Seaton, who started work as a cleaner of boilers and chimney flues, finds himself at fifteen in a cardboard factory 'lumping sacks of flour and alum from outside lorries to inside pastebins, or handing up trolley after trolley of wet fresh made cardboard in the stifling heat of the drying rooms' (Key: 212). Young workers may later move to more skilled jobs, learning to operate lathes or milling-machines for making precision parts or becoming welders, tool-setters or factory mechanics. But these positions require little more intellectual activity than the menial tasks of sweeping floors or carrying bobbins from one sewing machine to another, and despite the differing amounts of skill involved they are all characterised by tedious repetition. Jobs outside the factory, such as those of colliers and navvies, lavatory attendants and gas meter men, are similarly undemanding and monotonous.

The tedium and frustration endured by many of Sillitoe's

working-class men because of the nature of their jobs are reflected in the living habits of families, and are most noticeably evident in their wives' repetitive patterns of worry about 'making do' on limited incomes. The hardships of abject poverty experienced during the depression of the thirties are recalled by a number of characters in the early fiction. In the days when 'nearly all the kids in school ... [had] dads on dole', there was nothing unusual about Liza Atkin, the heroine of 'The Good Women', taking an old pram 'on to the rubbish and rammel tips to fill it by dusk with wood, old rags, or metal, in order to pull in a few bob a week and supplement the dole' (passim). Although some of Sillitoe's heroes (notably the Seaton brothers) make comparisons between these extremes of pre-war poverty and a relatively affluent present, financial problems persist and continue to plague most of his working-class families after the war. Brian Seaton recalls that the five-pound wage packet his father brought home just after the war made him better off than the thirty-eight shillings he sometimes earned during the depression, but a few years later the ten pounds a week earned by each of the Doddoe brothers in their fledgling scrap-metal business is insufficient to support their families. The most affluent characters in the post-war working-class world are young bachelors such as Arthur Seaton who hold skilled jobs in factories. They do not save their earnings, however, and one is led to assume that marriage will introduce them to the economic difficulties normally experienced by other members of their class. The continuing necessity for careful management of a man's wages is emphasised in 'The Magic Box', set in 1952, in which the husband turns over his wage packet each Friday night to his wife, whose 'skill at housekeeping demanded that each bob and tanner be accounted for. He would be laughed at by his workmates if they knew, though many of them lived by the same arrangement, and that was a fact' (RD : 68). Pre-war habits of running up grocery bills at local shops are still carried on in the post-war world of *Saturday Night and Sunday Morning* and *The Loneliness of the Long-Distance Runner*. And even the 'luxury' appliances such as washing machines and television sets that begin to appear in Sillitoe's working-class homes after the war are normally bought on hire-purchase schemes which extend payments over months and even years.

Watching the 'telly' offers Sillitoe's families one means of escape from the relatively dreary routines of their daily existence. A more significant activity in terms of class identification, however, is their habit of pubbing. The cliché that there are two classes of Englishmen, the public-school man and the public house man, is obviously an over-simplification. Nonetheless, the pub is the single most important point of reference outside the factory and the home in Sillitoe's description of working-class life. In the Nottingham fiction alone twenty-six of them are mentioned specifically, including The Horse and Groom, Flying Fox, Nottingham Rose, Peach Tree, Trip to Jerusalem, Plumtree, Red Dragon, Skittling Alley, John Barleycorn, Robin Hood Arms and The Jolly Higglers, and a good many more appear without names. The working man's 'local' or favourite pub offers him both an escape from the harsher aspects of working-class life and a reinforced sense of belonging to a particular social group. It is here he meets his friends, by design or chance, for in Sillitoe's early fiction visiting among working-class people is limited to relatives, children or courting couples. He may indulge in a pub crawl, taking a pint or more at each of a number of pubs within walking distance, like Harold Seaton does with his father-in-law or his son Arthur does with his cousins. Generally, however, he frequents a 'local' to discuss spectator sports such as football or racing, or to take part in long-running games of draughts, dominoes or darts.

Occasionally Sillitoe's women join one another in a pub for an enjoyable afternoon escape from their own particular worries. The narrator in 'The Good Women', for example, recalls his mother's return home after one such excursion: ' "We do have some bleddy fun, me and old Liza," she said on one of those rare evenings when she could hardly cook the old man's tea' (RD: 164). And if the Seaton family may be taken as typical, high points of social life for working-class families are frequently pub-centred. The victorious end of the Second World War is celebrated by them in a pub, Brian and Pauline hold their wedding reception at The Trafalgar, and the Christmas Day family get-together is climaxed by an evening at the 'local'. But the public house proclivities of Sillitoe's characters are most memorably captured when Harry, the narrator of 'The Fishing Boat Picture', points out his wife's most distinguishing feature, her frequent desire for 'a pint of beer and a quart of noise' (LLDR : 88).

Throughout the Nottingham fiction Sillitoe presents working-class characters who are strongly influenced by physical and economic pressures. Since their activities are restricted because of limited income, they are shown having a definite preference for the immediate and the local. They are portrayed as victims of continual noise and crowded living conditions, yet in the process of responding to these irritants they are able to achieve a strong sense of communal identity. The impression of working-class solidarity is reinforced in one story after another by Sillitoe's careful concentration on three common points of reference for their activities: home, factory and pub. While in the end there is no doubt that Sillitoe's focus is limited, within his self-imposed limitations he has nonetheless managed to create in the Nottingham fiction a consistent pattern of working-class activity that has a convincing ring of authenticity for the reader.

Notes and References

[1] Throughout the text the following abbreviations are used to indicate pagination for quotations from Sillitoe's fiction: SNSM: *Saturday Night and Sunday Morning*; LLDR : *The Loneliness of the Long-Distance Runner*; Key: *Key to the Door*; RD: *The Ragman's Daughter*; DWP: *The Death of William Posters*; TF: *A Tree on Fire*. Brief quotations in the same sentence from more than one work are indicated by 'passim'. Page references are to original editions, details of which are given in the bibliography.

Chapter Five

The Seeds of Dissent:
Significant Working-class Attitudes

In April, 1964, Alan Sillitoe published an article on working-class life in a special Nottingham issue of *Anarchy*, a limited circulation monthly, in which he attempted to analyse the psychology of being poor. The article ranged haphazardly over various working-class conditions and attitudes and finally came to focus on what Sillitoe sees as the central bias of working-class life: 'The poor know of only two classes in society. Their sociology is much simplified. There are *them* and *us*. Them are those who tell you what to do ... use a different accent ... pay your wages, collect rent ... hand you the dole or national assistance money ... live on your backs ... tread you down.' The assertion is familiar to readers of Sillitoe's early fiction, for expressions of a them–us mentality pervade the Nottingham novels and stories. In *Saturday Night and Sunday Morning*, *Key to the Door*, *The Loneliness of the Long-Distance Runner* and *The Ragman's Daughter* his characters normally define an allegiance to their own class (*us*) by expressing antipathy towards a broad spectrum of non-working-class individuals and institutions who are collectively referred to as *them*. *They* are frequently members or representatives of government or of a vaguely apprehended establishment characterised by their power to oppress the workers, to tell them 'what to do'. More specifically, *they* include politicians, policemen, commissioned ranks in the armed forces, landlords, school masters, factory bosses, means test men, doctors and office workers. Conflict with *them* is a working-class habit of mind, according to Sillitoe in this early work, and this belief finds widespread expression in the thoughts, words and actions of his characters.

Smith, the imprisoned protagonist in 'The Loneliness of the Long-Distance Runner', reflects on the division between *them* and *us* and easily convinces himself that 'they don't see eye to eye with us and we don't see eye to eye with them, so that's how it stands and how it will always stand' (LLDR : 8). Jogging alone over the early-morning countryside he hones his hatred to a fine point against 'cops, governors, posh whores, pen-pushers, army officers, [and] Members of Parliament', grouping them together as 'In-law blokes like you and them, all on the watch for Out-law blokes like me and us – waiting to phone for the coppers as soon as we make a false move' (LLDR : 10, 15). The sense of paranoia in evidence here is echoed in Smith's feeling of injustice at being incarcerated for stealing about a hundred and fifty pounds from a baker's shop; and he decides that 'by sending me to Borstal they've shown me the knife, and from now on ... it's war between me and them ... now they've shown me the knife, whether I ever pinch another thing in my life again or not, I know who my enemies are' (LLDR : 16). Inequities in the distribution of wealth, the obvious gulf between the possessors of property, position and power and the working-class, have given Smith both target and weapon in his war against *them*. His attitude is shared by Tony, a convicted thief and narrator of 'The Ragman's Daughter', who steals regularly from his employer despite having a prison record. He refuses to steal simply for 'kicks', and although he credits himself with a long series of apparently successful thefts, he dreams of living 'in a country where I didn't like thieving and where I didn't want to thieve, a place where everybody felt the same way because they all had only the same as everyone else – even if it wasn't much' (RD: 10). A similar utopian fantasy is expressed by Brian Seaton, who theorises that 'the wealth of the world should be pooled and divided fairly among those

who worked, doctors and labourers, architects and mechanics' (Key: 439). Although he does not attempt to redress
working-class grievances about social injustices by stealing
from those who are better off than he is or who have power
over him, Brian nevertheless nurtures an emotional and spiritual rebellion which affects all his relationships with *them* and
allows him to assert with pride at the end of the novel: 'I
ain't let the bastards grind me down' (Key: 445). (The statement is an echo, or a response, to his brother Arthur's caution
in *Saturday Night and Sunday Morning*: 'Don't let the bastards
grind you down' (38).) Arthur Seaton feels that rebelling
against institutions that oppress the workers is both necessary
and inevitable. He claims 'it's best to be a rebel so as to show
'em it don't pay to try to do you down. Factories and labour
exchanges and insurance offices keep us alive and kicking –
so they say – but they're booby-traps and will suck you under
like sinking-sands if you aren't careful. Factories sweat you
to death, insurance and income tax offices milk money from
your wage packets and rob you to death. And if you're still
left . . . after all this boggering about, the army calls you up
and you get shot to death' (SNSM: 196). For Arthur, and
for so many of Sillitoe's other characters, 'it's a hard life if
you don't weaken'; but weakening is not to be thought of
in the world of the Nottingham fiction, for it means giving
them the opportunity of 'grinding your face in the muck'
(SNSM: 196).

The roots of conflict lie deep in Sillitoe's working-class
families, and children learn at an early age to mock and fight
against the opposing forces of *them*. The most obvious childhood adversaries are teachers and police. Brian Seaton recalls
that his school headmaster, Mr Jones, 'was enemy number
one, a white-haired tod who stalked the corridors during
school hours' sadistically dealing out undeserved punish-
ments (Key: 116). Brian also remembers how his aunt Ada
burst into a classroom one morning to punch a teacher in
the face for having made a slighting remark the day before
to her son Johnny for wearing hand-me-down woman's
clothing. Tony tells in 'The Ragman's Daughter' of reacting

against a classroom lesson in buying and selling because he wasn't given enough coins to satisfy his needs by the 'plummy' voiced teacher. And young Bert Doddoe is taught by his father that teachers are as contemptible as 'coppers' because they're 'all part of the gov'ment' (Key: 156). While school-teachers are recognised as natural enemies by Sillitoe's working-class children, 'coppers' are generally hated even more. In the Nottingham fiction parental and sibling examples frequently lead children to experiments in aggression. Consequent and inevitable brushes with the law quickly teach the young offenders that policemen are antagonists to be mistrusted, hated and feared. Bert Doddoe is undeterred when 'copper's narks' send his 'elder brother to approved school after knocking the living daylights out of him so he'd tell them where he hid the gas-meter money', and is later sent to approved school himself 'for lifting bicycle lamps' (Key: 116, 169). Their brother Johnny is put on probation for two years when he is caught after stealing a bicycle. But as Brian Seaton tells Bert, the condition is not abnormal: 'a lot o' my pals is on probation' (Key: 110). Even though initial skirmishes with the police are 'touch and go, like kittens, like boxing-gloves, like dobbie', as Smith explains in 'The Loneliness of the Long-Distance Runner', most of the children in the early fiction believe that 'coppers is bastards' (passim). Even the escapist fantasies of these children incorporate challenges to police authority. The narrator in 'The Disgrace of Jim Scarfedale' tells himself: 'As soon as I see a way of making off – even if I have to rob meters to feed myself – I'll take it'; and the narrator of 'The Good Women' recalls a childhood plan to run away with his pal and 'live like bandits', 'pinching' things to stay alive (passim). Brian Seaton, who tells his brothers and sisters a bedtime story filled with violence, robbery and murder, has his hatred for the police reinforced by *Les Misérables*, which he reads as the history of a common man who was unjustly 'hounded by the police' to his death (Key: 193).

Childhood skirmishes with teachers and policemen, however, are merely preparation for the more extended conflicts with *them* carried on by Sillitoe's adolescents and adults. Life for them consists in large part of coping with a never-ending series of threats to their peace of mind or physical well-being. While these threats may be real or imagined, they nonetheless carry considerable weight in working-class perceptions of reality. Generally they are associated with menacing representatives of some external authority such as landlords, gaffers (bosses) or policemen. Confrontations may be direct or indirect, sometimes resulting in verbal or physical battles between one of *them* and one of *us*, sometimes recorded as a silent or verbalised damnation of *their* policies or actions. If there is one common element in these outbursts, it lies in the sense of persecution which motivates them, a widely-held belief that *they* are pursuing a policy of unjustified enmity and harassment aimed directly against members of the working-class.

Chapter Four described the 'bug-eaten back-to-backs' near the factories where most of Sillitoe's Nottingham characters live. These buildings are generally run down, whether they are owned by municipal corporations or individuals, and the unwillingness of the landlords to make necessary repairs is often matched by the stubbornness of the tenants. The Doddoes, for example, left their back door 'slightly ajar day and night for years because the landlord wouldn't repair the uneven floor tiles' (SNSM: 70). Arthur Seaton complains about lack of repairs in his parents' home 'even though they pay the rent', and refers contemptuously to the rent collector as a 'swivel-eyed swine' (SNSM: 128). Other families simply don't pay rent, and a strike inciter at one of the factories can count on enthusiastic response when he urges non-payment of rent during a proposed strike: 'Don't forget there are ten thousand of us at this factory, and if [the landlords] want our families as well on the street, let's see 'em put us there' (RD: 178).

Inside the factories feelings run high against the 'gaffers', a term applied by the workers to anyone with power to tell them what to do, from foreman to factory owner. Few of Sillitoe's characters admit to liking their jobs, though some, such as Arthur Seaton and Liza Atkin, harbour ambivalent attitudes about them. On the one hand Liza is said to have 'enjoyed every one of the thousands' of steel elbows she had to check each day with a test gauge, because 'it implied so much trust in her' (RD: 173). On the other hand, she resented 'the gaffers in their big cars' and 'felt good, being on strike; it was a way of doing damage to those who bossed the world about' (RD: 182). Arthur Seaton could work his lathe while dreaming of life outside factory walls: 'if your machine was working well . . . and you sprung your actions into a favourable rhythm you became happy. You went off into pipe-dreams for the rest of the day' (SNSM: 37). Yet he was offended by the foreman's close watch on him, and had violent fantasies of blowing up the factory and then laughing 'at the wonderful sight of gaffers and machines and shining bikes going sky-high one wonderful moonlit night' (SNSM: 38). For some workers, such as Brian Seaton, the villains are factory owners: one of them is 'a Bible-backed slave driver', while the others only want 'higher production and more money in their pockets' (Key: 249, 255). He recalls with particular distaste the situation at Robinson's cardboard factory where 'you could be sure of being kept on for as long as you worked like a slave and touched your cap to the gaffers every time you passed. It was one of those firms that had a tradition of benevolence behind it, meaning hard work and little pay to the right sort of people – those who would serve the firm through their thick and your thin' (Key: 248). His bitterness is marked as he remembers how 'wage rates at Robinson's had been carefully regulated – set at a fraction above the dole money, enough to give the incentive of a regular job, but hardly enough to keep its employees far from a harrowing experience in near starvation' (Key: 249).

For many other workers condemned to a 'factory incarceration' it is the foreman who represents *them*, and is therefore the object of intense dislike. Vera Seaton remembers long hours in a factory before her marriage, 'working at looms and threading bobbins, slaving under the fore-woman's eye' (Key: 37). Liza Atkin tells of a supposedly

birthplace: 38 Manton Crescent, Nottingham. *Below:* Beaco[...]
The Raleigh Bicycle factory is on the far left.

friendly foreman who would whistle before approaching a work area 'so that work could be resumed before he showed his face. One day he didn't give his customary warning and two women were sacked' (RD: 176). No such reminder of a foreman's allegiance to *them* is needed by Arthur Seaton, who has been taught by his father to regard him as 'the enemy's scout' (SNSM: 61). When Arthur receives his weekly pay from Robboe, the bicycle factory foreman, he considers the encounter a kind of truce: 'though no strong cause for open belligerence existed as in the bad old days ... [before the war] it persisted for more subtle reasons that could hardly be understood but were nevertheless felt, and Friday afternoon was a time when different species met beneath white flags, with wage-packets as mediators' (SNSM: 61). Robboe is further alienated by owning an ageing car and 'a semi-detached in a posh district, and Arthur held these pretensions against him because basically they were of equal stock' (SNSM: 40). It is clear, to the Seatons at least, that the factory foreman who aligns himself with *them* in job and imitation lifestyle must necessarily forfeit the friendship of his fellow workers.

Reference has been made to Brian Seaton's bitterness about the subservient manner a working man had to assume to keep his job before the war. Other characters, in stories set before and after the war, voice similar views. In each case it is the bosses' power of abrupt and unjustified dismissal that the workers find intolerable. In the thirties the Seaton boys' uncle Doddoe loses his job as a collier 'for cursing at the overseer down pit' (Key: 59). In the story 'To Be Collected', set in the early post-war years, three labourers save their money and buy an old lorry to use collecting scrap metal. When one of them complains about the low initial income from the business, he is quickly reminded of the insecurity of 'working for a bleeding gaffer ... you've only got to pull out a fag and you get your cards. Or [leave the premises to] see whether or not you backed a winner at dinnertime' (RD: 120).

The sense of persecution exhibited in working-class references to gaffers also marks their relationships with the police. Derogatory references to 'coppers' pepper Sillitoe's early fiction and reveal the fear, sensitivity to unfairness and sheer hatred felt by his characters. In 'The Loneliness of the Long-Distance Runner' Smith remarks that 'it's a good life ... if you don't give in to coppers and Borstal bosses and the rest of them bastard-faced In-laws' (LLDR: 11–12). This view is shared by the narrator of 'The Bike', who unknowingly buys a stolen bicycle from a fellow worker named Bernard. He is later arrested for 'being found with a pinched bike ... [and is] put on probation' (RD: 111). Yet although he can 'hate old Bernard's guts for playing a trick like that on me, his mate', he cannot turn him in, because 'I hated the coppers more and wouldn't nark on anybody, not even a dog' (RD: 111). Smith himself also tells of a 'copper' who comes to question him about a robbery. The policeman is not asked into Smith's home, however, for such an invitation 'would seem more suspicious than keeping him outside, because they know we hate their guts and smell a rat if they think we're trying to be nice to them' (LLDR: 30). The pervasiveness of this aggressive attitude is shown in various working-class encounters with the police. The recently arrested narrator of 'The Good Women', for example, tells of 'how a Nottingham pal ... had been stopped for driving a lorry without a rear light. My pal hadn't known about it, but the cop was going to book him anyway, so his long arm shot from the cab and the cop went flying against a wall' (RD: 147). In 'To Be Collected' the sight of a policeman provokes a violent fantasy in the mind of Bert, an ex-collier: 'I'd like to build eight machine-guns into this vehicle ... to blast coppers, that's what I'd use it for. ... One 'ud put his hand out to get my licence ... six on 'em at a roadblock. ... So I'd press this specially built-in button, and hear them bullet-belts starting to move under our feet, and the road in front would get churned up ... and the lorry would go bump-bump over the rubble we'd made of everything, and we'd laugh together at six coppers snuffing it behind' (RD: 117). Such violence is explicable in Sillitoe's fictional world: in the same way that stealing from *them* carries no social disapproval

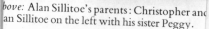

bove: Alan Sillitoe's parents: Christopher and
an Sillitoe on the left with his sister Peggy.

Above: Alan Sillitoe'
Terrace, Nottingham.

Chapter Nine.

The following week, when Jack was on days, he walked over to the Nursery, to see Arthur. Jack seemed to have shrunk to no size at all in the last month. He was sallow at the face, his lips were always halfopen as if he were talking to himself, and his black hair that Arthur remembered so glossy was now dead and lifeless and receding at the temples. Arthur had a good idea what it was that Jack was coming to see him about. He stood by his machine and watched him come into the shop looking as though he had no right there. He nodded briefly to Jack the foreman and made his way through the gangways of machines towards Arthur.

But Arthur was in trouble because too many people had been talking about him. Em'ler had blabbed, and so had the neighbours who lived around Winnie. Only Em'ler and Jack knew what happened when Arthur made his way out of the house by the back door last Monday night. Arthur tried to imagine the scene when Em'ler finally let Jack into the living room, littered with wet towels, empty glasses & gin bottles, and the centre of the room taken up by a long zinc bath of water still steaming. What had she said? He would liked to have been an invisible listener. Now that Jack had come halfway across the factory to see him he would find out what had happened. He had seen Brenda since, but she did not know. Though the gin and hot bath had been successful she did not say much to Arthur, sitting glumly with him in the Royal Children and being sarcastic when she spoke. As for Winnie, he felt sorry now for what have happened to her: he could imagine clearly what had happened. Brenda in her morose way had given him a hint of it. Bill had arrived from Germany. The same night he went to the beer-off at the end of the street, and stood talking to one of the tight-lipped women that passed for neighbours, who lost no time in saying what a good woman Winnie had been while Bill was away, yet at the same time hinting that something fishy had been going on the night before, and adding that Winnie had been seen in the "Peach Tree" with a young chap who was tall and had fair hair. In the quarrel and knocking around that took place when Bill got back to the house, Winnie ended up with a black eye and Bill with the claw marks of a tiger down one side of his face, and Winnie admitted that of course she had been in the Peach Tree with Arthur, but that he was waiting to see Brenda her sister, who had turned up after only ten minutes,

A page from the first draft of the manuscript of *Saturday Night and Sunday Morning*.

Top: Alan Sillitoe (left) when serving as a wireless operator in Malaya, with Bill Brown from Newcastle. *Centre:* Alan Sillitoe and Ruth Fainlight in Soller, Majorca, 1956. *Bottom:* Alan Sillitoe in 1978.

because of *their* exploitation of the working-class, so frustrating *their* agents the police by whatever means possible is felt to be legitimate and desirable action.

Reactions to police intervention in their lives vary a great deal for Sillitoe's characters. The narrator of 'The Good Women' recalls how he learned as a child that the police were 'to fear and look out for' (RD: 147). The adolescent Smith, despite his bravado when questioned at home by a policeman, expects an interrogation at headquarters to be more brutal. He tells of being threatened on one occasion by a 'dirty bullying jumped-up bastard' in uniform: ' "Listen, my lad," he said ... "I don't want too much of your lip, because if we get you down to the Guildhall you'll get a few bruises and black eyes for your trouble." And I knew he wasn't kidding either, because I'd heard about all them sort of tricks' (LLDR: 33). Smith's fears of 'them sort of tricks', it will be recalled, echo Bert Doddoe's comments on his brother's experience of police brutality after his arrest. Liza Atkin, in her forties after the war and on strike from the factory where she works, worries about 'coppers' being used as strike breakers. Tony in 'The Ragman's Daughter' looks up apprehensively at the 'night of open sky with a million ears and eyes of copper stars cocked and staring' before committing the robbery for which he is later caught and convicted (RD: 27). The narrator of 'The Good Women' resigns himself to being arrested when he has counted 'the immediate members of ... [his] family who had been inside, and got as far as nine' (RD: 146). Ernest Brown, the lonely, ageing upholsterer and protagonist in 'Uncle Ernest', is harassed by plain clothes detectives when he befriends two undernourished young girls. Giving them meals and small gifts at the cafe where he normally eats, he grows dependent on their company and comes to feel 'these two girls whom he looked upon almost as his own daughters were the only people he had to love' (LLDR: 64). The police, however, misinterpret his friendliness towards the children and force him to give them up. Filled with hatred and self-pity at his victimisation, he drinks himself into oblivion.

The passivity shown by Ernest Brown is rare among Sillitoe's characters. Generally they react much more belligerently when threatened by *them*, whether they are directly
involved in a personal confrontation or finding themselves
affected by the impersonal procedures of government. In the
latter case they denounce even the most ordinary powers of
government, such as levying and collecting taxes, enforcing
law and order and waging war, for they consider the exercise
of such powers to be further efforts by *them* to 'live on your
backs ... [to] tread you down.' The anti-government attitudes of Arthur Seaton are typical of those held by other principal characters in the early fiction. Like his brother Brian,
Arthur sees Nottingham Castle as a despised symbol of
government because of its use as a prison for deserters during
the war, and he fantasises about destroying it: 'he turned
around and saw the squat front-end of the castle still sneering
at him. I hate that castle, he said to himself, more than I've
ever hated owt in my life before, and I'd like to plant a thousand tons of bone-dry TNT in the tunnel called Mortimer's
Hole and send it to Kingdom Cum' (SNSM: 70). He also
talks about his lifelong fight against law and order and claims
that government's 'looney laws' are made 'to be broken by
blokes like me' (SNSM: 34). At the end of the novel he feels
there is 'still the vast crushing power of government against
which to lean his white-skinned bony shoulder, a thousand
of its laws to be ignored and therefore broken' (SNSM: 198).
But unlike other protagonists such as Smith and Tony,
Arthur talks more about breaking laws than actually committing the acts, and at times his diatribes seem awkwardly
conceived and have a hollow ring, such as when he speaks
of 'striving to kick down his enemies crawling like ants over
the capital letter G of Government' (SNSM: 198). Yet his
sense of persecution is real enough: he worries about being
able to enjoy 'some of the sweet and agreeable things of life
... before Government destroyed him', and complains about
the unfair burden of taxes (SNSM: 198). 'Just look what the
sods do to me', he grumbles on receiving his weekly wage
packet, 'Income Tax, two pounds eighteen and a tanner. It

ain't right. That's munney I've earned. I know what I'd like to do wi' 'em' (SNSM: 59). His mother reinforces this view when she refers colourfully to paying taxes as 'feeding pigs on cherries' (SNSM: 30).

Arthur's personal aversion to army duty provides another useful focus on the hostility Sillitoe's working-class men exhibit against *them*: 'When I'm on my fifteen-days' training and I lay on my guts behind a sandbag shooting at a target board I know whose faces I've got in my sights every time the new rifle cracks off. Yes. The bastards that put the gun into my hands. I make up a quick picture of their stupid four-eyed faces that blink as they read big books and papers on how to get blokes into khaki and fight battles in a war that they'll never be in – and then I let fly at them. Crack-crack-crack-crack-crack-crack' (SNSM: 128). The intensity of Arthur's antipathy towards 'the bastards that put the gun into my hands' is a Seaton family tradition. Eddie Seaton, his uncle, deserted from the army in 1917, though he was caught and sent to France a few months later. His father Harold, bitter from long years of unemployment during the thirties which he blamed on government policies, got himself classified as medically unfit for service when he 'swung the lead a bit' about his eyesight. As he explains his position: 'after all them years on the dole I swore I'd never fayt for 'em, the bleddy bastards. Not after all me and yer mam and yo' lot 'ad ter put up wi'' (Key: 218). When Arthur is conscripted after the war and ironically put in the military police because of his height, he comforts himself with subversive thoughts: 'Let them start a war ... and see what a bad soldier I can be. "Them at the top" must know that nobody would fight, and he supposed that because of this they weren't so anxious to rely on them in another war' (SNSM: 128). And although Brian Seaton voluntarily joins the Air Force to see the world, he soon grows disenchanted with service life. Finding himself 'lassoed from left and right by legislation devised by some genius for persecution', he sees his identity card as 'a convict passport' and himself as 'a prisoner' who is 'slave-laboured' into duties he detests' (Key: passim).

Arthur's relatives and peers, who are usually conscripted and serve as privates – a rank which parallels their social position in the civilian world – share his anger against *their* power to wage war by imposing compulsory military service. They frequently go to some trouble to dissociate themselves from the forces, either by evading the call-up or by deserting once they are inducted. Between the wars young Brian Seaton encounters an emotionally-disturbed veteran named Agger, who has lost 'his faith in guidance from the men "above" him' because of 'the useless slaughter of employable sinews' in the First World War (Key: 76). As a result he feels it his duty to caution others to 'on'y join up when they stop the dole and chuck us off these bleeding premises' (Key: 77). This kind of advice is certainly heeded by the Seatons, for during the second war 'out of a dozen able-bodied men in all remotely connected branches of the family, only two went into the army and stayed, and one was killed in Tunisia' (Key: 258). Arthur particularly remembers 'the return of [his aunt] Ada's three sons after their short terms of army service at the beginning of the war' and sympathises with these 'tall, grinning deserters [who were] caught time and again by Redcaps or police, but always escaping, on the run, in hiding, living with whores, thieving for food and money because they had neither ration-books nor employment cards' (SNSM: 72, 126). The persistence of another deserter is recounted in 'To Be Collected', in which a gunner named Donnie Hodson 'came [home] on leave one day and never went back' (RD: 124). Though he is caught, 'it was still the middle of the war when they let him out of jail and turned him over to the redcaps, so he hopped it a second time, and uniform number two burst into paraffin-flame from the bedroom grate' (RD: 126). And the narrator in 'The Good Women' tells of another gunner called Robert the Welshman who 'slipped through the barbed wire' of an AA battery near Nottingham and was sheltered by Liza Atkin until he was caught and later 'killed on a convoy going to Archangel' (RD: 158, 163).

The widespread unwillingness of these working-class men to take part in 'government' wars underlines their mental habit of associating government with *them*. *They* 'tell you what to do' and so does the army; *they* try to 'grind you down' and wars give them additional opportunity to do so. In particular Sillitoe's characters cherish a notion that *they* make huge wartime profits out of working-class suffering, and hint at nefarious collusion between politicians and establishment businessmen. In 'To Be Collected' Donnie Hodson and a housewife talk disdainfully about fighting for powerful schemers who care nothing about ordinary people 'as long as they fill their own pockets' (RD: 123). In *Key to the Door* Brian Seaton talks about Churchill's conduct of the war: 'He didn't give a bogger about us. It was all his bleeding factory-owners he saved, the jumped-up bags like owd Edgeworth who's making a fortune' (Key: 366). And in 'Noah's Ark' two small boys named Bert and Colin echo sentiments taught them by Bert's father as they chant

> We don't want to charge with the
> fusiliers
> Bomb with the bombardiers
> Fight with the racketeers
> We want to stay at home
>
> We don't want to fight in a Tory war
> Die like the lads before
> Drown in the mud and gore
> We want to go to work
> (LLDR: 116).

Working-class hostility is directed against the Tories or Conservatives in much of Sillitoe's early fiction. Whether they are conducting wars, exercising power in other ways, or merely canvassing support for an upcoming election, Conservative politicians are constantly derided by the workers. There are individual attacks on political leaders: Chamberlain is mocked for his well-known 'peace in our time' statement, and Churchill is referred to as 'old Fatguts' throughout *Key to the Door* and remembered as one of the 'gang as turned hose pipes on the hunger marchers before the war' (Key: passim). There is also more general condemnation, such as Arthur Seaton's railing against 'these big fat Tory bastards in Parliament ... [who] rob our wage packets every week with insurance and income tax and tell us it's for our own good' (SNSM: 34). (Arthur's protest is not only directed against Conservatives; he also takes a shot at 'them Labour bleeders too' in a blanket condemnation of all politicians.) Brian Seaton recalls his father saying that 'coppers' and schoolteachers are 'all Conservatives' and warning him 'if ever yer vote conservative ... I'll smash yer brains out' (Key: 156). Brian knows that 'millionaires vote Conservative', and by associating the word with *them* he concludes that 'Conservative ... was an official word to be distrusted, hated in fact' (Key: 157). Similar distrust is evident in a speech made by the leader of a wildcat strike of factory hands in 'The Good Women' when he damns 'the Tory press and the Tory union bosses [for] trying to kid' the workers about their position (RD: 185). And Smith in 'The Loneliness of the Long-Distance Runner' remembers mocking 'some Tory [on television] telling us about how good his government was going to be if we kept on voting for them – their slack chops rolling, opening and bumbling, hands lifting to twitch moustaches and touching their buttonholes to make sure the flower hadn't wilted, so that you could see they didn't mean a word they said' (LLDR: 22).

Generally Sillitoe's characters align themselves politically with Labour. In *Key to the Door* working-class adolescents 'who snubbed any suggestion of joining a cadet force yet wanted to meet friends once a week' congregate at a local club supported by the Labour party (Key: 363). Brian Seaton thinks about politics and decides that 'Labour was the best thing', a decision influenced by his father, who was 'red Labour', and no doubt also by 'the solid bloc of anarchistic Labour [voters] in the street' where the Seatons lived (passim). There is also a certain sympathy for the Communists in the Nottingham fiction. Abb Fowler, a friend of Harold Seaton, is a Communist, as is Ernie in 'The Other

John Peel'. Arthur Seaton resists easy classification: on the one hand he protests 'I ain't a Communist, I tell you. I like 'em though'; yet he votes Communist illegally on his bedridden father's voting card because 'I allus like to 'elp the losin' side' (SNSM: 33–34). Arthur's sympathy for the losing side may be a natural outgrowth of working-class feelings of resentment at being perpetual underdogs in society; and this may also account for Brian Seaton's 'half facetious and serious' claim to be a Communist while he is fighting Communist guerilla action in Malaya. The romantic Brian, however, is more accurately pigeon-holed as a 'socialist-anarchist' by one of his more politically astute acquaintances, a Canadian corporal named Len Knotman.

The political alignment of Sillitoe's workers – against a traditional Tory association with power and privilege; for an assumed egalitarianism in Labour and Communist creeds – mirrors their interpretation of English society. In a social world sharply divided between *them* and *us*, members of the working-class see themselves rejected, exploited and persecuted. In a world dominated by *them*, they constantly search for ways to redress the balance. As we have seen, principal characters in a number of the Nottingham stories, including Smith and Tony, feel justified in stealing from *them* and frustrating *their* agents, the police, whenever the opportunity presents itself. Both Arthur Seaton and Liza Atkin support industrial unrest, frustrating the planned-profit formulas of factory owners and bosses. Harold Seaton, along with numerous relatives and others such as Donnie Hodson, rejects and avoids compulsory service in the armed forces. And Brian Seaton devotes a good deal of his energy to castigating past and present power élites and dreaming about the achievement of a new social order.

By and large, however, the characters in Sillitoe's early fiction remain incipient revolutionaries, aware of the need for drastic social reform but unable or unwilling to commit themselves fully to it. The rhetoric of revolution may be found throughout the Nottingham novels and stories, but it usually takes the form of simplistic theorising or fantasised projections of violent retribution to be meted out to *them*. In 'The Disgrace of Jim Scarfedale' Jim's wife 'used to talk about politics ... [when he came home from work at the factory] saying how the world was made for blokes like me and that we should run the world and not leave it to a lot of money-grabbing capitalist bastards' (LLDR : 149). Liza Atkin listens sympathetically to a strike leader's speech: 'Well, they can give us what we want in this dispute ... and they can give us a raise when we force the boggers to it, but as far as I'm concerned ... it's not a raise here and a bit of an improvement there that we want ... it's a whole bloody change ... a turnover from top to bottom' (RD: 179). Liza reflects later that the strike 'wasn't total or decisive enough ... such a downing of tools as had taken place meant little because instead of coming back to work they should have stayed and gone on from there' (RD: 186). Liza's intuitive feeling that a workers' revolution is likely to happen is shared by various characters in the early fiction, including Arthur Seaton and Ernie in 'The Other John Peel'. Ernie has even chosen his weapon, a ·303 rifle like the one his friend Bob stole from army stores: 'Just the thing to have in case of a revolution. I hope I can get my hands on one when the trouble starts' (RD: 41). Others, such as the narrator in 'The Bike' and Smith, speculate on the possibilities of revenge against *them* once it is achieved. Smith fantasises about the Borstal warden's death, and he dreams of having the 'whip-hand' when he can take 'all the cops, governors, posh whores, pen-pushers, army officers, Members of Parliament ... stick them up against a wall and let them have it' (LLDR: 15).

Belief in the possible achievement of an egalitarian social order, and contemplation of revenge against those who control the present one, may be considered spiritual resources which Sillitoe's working-class people draw on in the Nottingham fiction to mitigate the physical and psychological pressures afflicting them. Ironically their habitual concern with the immediate and momentary aspects of perennial confrontation with *them* allows only a tentative approach to the larger issue of 'a whole bloody change'. In the Nottingham fiction the lines of battle are clearly drawn, but the characters must content themselves with small triumphs, with temporary and individual successes in skirmishes with *them*. It is only later, in the first two novels of the trilogy (and to a limited extent in the third), that Sillitoe's protagonists take more positive action to implement the social utopia of their dreams.

Chapter Six

Touchstones of Reality:
Meeting Points of Art and Life in the Early Fiction

Critical readers generally accept the novelist's right to select and shape the raw material of life for artistic purposes. When a novel purports to be a reflection of contemporary society, however, the reader has a right to expect a recognisable picture. The novelist's selective emphasis on certain aspects of that society may not suit the reader's sense of decorum or perspective, but so long as there is no gross distortion of the world he can test with his senses, he is willing to accept the credibility of the fictional milieu. If the novelist wishes to go a step further and draw attention to imperfections in society, he must be particularly careful to represent conditions as they actually exist, otherwise the knowledgeable reader will be little inclined to entertain his suggestions for their improvement. It is therefore of some importance in an assessment of Alan Sillitoe, whose early work deplores injustices visited on the English working class by an uncaring society, that we attempt to establish the degree of accuracy with which he relates his fictional world to life.

The Industrial Revolution left England, particularly the northern half, with a heritage of slum housing. As recently as 1964 Donald Read pointed out that 'of fifty national slum blackspots forty-five are in the North', including areas around Leeds, Liverpool, Manchester, Nottingham, Sheffield and Hull.[1] In many industrial areas cheaply built houses dating from the eighteen-seventies are still lived in by working-class families, and conditions parallel those described in Sillitoe's early fiction. Richard Hoggart contends in *The Uses of Literacy* that working-class people 'have their own recognisable part of the towns, [and also that] they have, almost city by city, their own recognisable styles of housing.' He cites districts in Leeds (Hunslet), Manchester (Ancoats), Sheffield (Brightside and Attercliffe) and Hull (off the Hessle and Holderness Roads) as examples, and might have included Radford and the Alfreton Road area in Nottingham as well. Sociologists such as Madeline Kerr in *The People of Ship Street* and Michael Young and Peter Willmott in *Family and Kinship in East London* describe similar areas in other major centres.

General impressions of working-class areas are seldom described in pleasant terms. Hoggart writes of 'miles of smoking and huddled working-class houses'; Kerr tells us that 'the houses...are decrepit and dreary'; and George Orwell in *The Road to Wigan Pier* recalls 'labyrinths of little brick houses blackened by smoke, festering in planless chaos round miry alleys and little cindered yards.' Specifically, many observers refer to typical configurations of working-class houses known to readers of Sillitoe's fiction as 'two up and two down' and 'back to backs'. As Young and Willmott point out, many working-class homes share a single plan: 'on the first floor two bedrooms, and on the ground floor a living room, a kitchen and a small scullery.' 'Little four-room houses', D. H. Lawrence calls them in 'Nottingham and the Mining Country', 'with the "front" looking outward into the grim, blank street, and the "back", with a tiny square brick yard, a low wall, and a w.c. and ash-pit.' The inconvenience caused by a lack of indoor plumbing in the 'two up and two down' houses is aggravated in the 'back to backs', as George Orwell makes clear in his explanation of the term: '"Back to back" houses are two houses built in one, each side of the house being somebody's front door.... The front houses give on the street and the back ones on the yard, and there is only one way out of each house.... The lavatories are in the yard at the back, so that if you live on the side facing the street, to get to the lavatory or the dust-bin you have to go out of the front door and walk round the end of the block – a distance that may be as much as two hundred yards; if you live at the back, on the other hand, your outlook is on to a row of lavatories.' Yet another disadvantage of this type of housing, as Lewis Mumford notes in *The Culture of Cities*, is that 'two rooms out of four on each floor . . . [have] no direct daylight or ventilation.'

Sillitoe's characters not only have to put up with the in-convenience inherent in the kind of houses they inhabit, they must also learn to live in an unpleasant, unwholesome environment. In particular, various studies point to the high levels of noise and smoke pollution from nearby factories. Hoggart observes, for example, that working-class houses are often 'fitted into the dark and lowering canyons between the giant factories and the services which attend them; "the barracks of an industry" the Hammonds called them. . . . All day and all night the noises and smells of the district – factory hooters, trains shunting, the stink of the gas-works – remind you that life is a matter of shifts and clockings-in-and-out'. Echoing this is Mumford's description of houses 'built smack up against a steel works, a dye plant, a gas works, or a railroad cutting. They would be built often enough on land filled in with ashes and broken glass and rubbish, where even the grass could not take root; they might be on the edge of a dump or a vast permanent pile of coal and slag: day in and day out the stench of the refuse, the murky outpouring of chimneys, the noise of hammering or of whirring machinery, accom-panied household routine.'

There is a striking resemblance between these passages and the observations made by Sillitoe's characters noted in Chapter Four. In 'The Disgrace of Jim Scarfedale', for example, the reader will recall how the narrator 'could hear the engines and pulleys next door in the factory thumping away, and iron-presses slamming as if they were trying to burst through the wall and set up another department at the Scarfedales.' And in *Saturday Night and Sunday Morning* 'disinfectant-suds, grease, and newly-cut steel permeated the

air over the suburb of four-roomed houses' where the Seatons live; 'generators whined all night, and during the day
giant milling-machines working away on cranks and pedals
in the turnery gave to the terrace a sensation of living within
breathing distance of some monstrous being that suffered
from a disease of the stomach'. The resonant echoes set up
by these passages offer compelling evidence of accuracy in
Sillitoe's fictional record of living conditions in Nottingham's working-class slums.[2]

In *The Road to Wigan Pier* Orwell observes that scores of
thousands of condemned 'back to backs' remained inhabited
during the thirties simply because there was nothing better
available. 'In the industrial areas the mere difficulty of getting
hold of a house is one of the worst aggravations of poverty.
It means that people will put up with anything – any hole
and corner slum, any misery of bugs and rotting floors and
cracking walls, any extortion of skinflint landlords and black-
mailing agents – simply to get a roof over their heads. . . .
Some people hardly seem to realise that such things as decent
houses exist and look on bugs and leaking roofs as acts of
God; others rail bitterly against their landlords; but all cling
desperately to their houses lest worse should befall.' While
Sillitoe's detailed evocations of the hardships created by this
situation (especially in *Saturday Night and Sunday Morning* and
Key to the Door) are like Orwell's assessment of conditions,
his characters are capable of reacting more positively than
Orwell's passive workers. As Robert Roberts points out in
The Classic Slum: Salford Life in the first quarter of the century,
there is a well-established way of escaping both long overdue
rent payment and intolerably decrepit slum housing. Roberts
refers to the 'moonlight flit' 'when a whole household, to
dodge its debts, would vanish overnight. Everybody laughed
about it except the creditors.' Sillitoe's awareness of this
tradition is evident in *Key to the Door* when he has Harold
and Vera Seaton arrange 'a moonlight flit . . . for the darkest
night of the month according to Old Moore' (Key: 14). The
Seatons' flit is made from a bug-ridden condemned house in
Albion Yard, soon after 'the living room ceiling of the house

next door collapsed at four o'clock one morning', to 'an equally decrepit but not yet condemned house on Mount Street' (Key: 13).

Generally, however, Sillitoe's characters live in the same area and sometimes on the same street for long periods of their lives, sharing a proclivity to 'stay put' with their real-life counterparts. Madeline Kerr speaks of 'the genuine Ship Street resident', for example, whose family has been living there for two or three generations. Young and Willmott note a similar longevity in the 'turnings' or working-class streets covered in their study. And Richard Hoggart, describing his own family background in some detail, recalls that grandparents moved from open countryside in the eighteen-seventies and were packed into 'raw cheap housing' in 'inadequately cleansed and lighted' streets near a steelworks, where the family has remained ever since. Hoggart's testimony is particularly interesting, since his own family history is a close parallel to that of the Seatons, which Sillitoe develops in the Nottingham novels. Brian Jackson has suggested in *Working Class Community: Some general notions raised by a series of studies in northern England* that 'the working-class family is less mobile ... than others [because] their jobs, opportunities and aspirations make them stick to the local scene.' Madeline Kerr has come to a similar conclusion, finding that many working-class families *prefer* to remain where they are, that long-term familiarity with people and events on a particular street is not only the only life they know, but 'the only one they want to know.' David Downes, in *The Delinquent Solution: A Study in Subcultural Theory*, feels compelled to quote from Kerr's study, noting 'an overt preference for slum-dwelling' by socially underprivileged families whose circumstances are much like those of Sillitoe's characters. As Young and Willmott conclude in their report on East London: 'dilapidated but cosy, damp but friendly, in the eye of most Bethnal Greeners these [1870's] cottages are the [best] place' to live.

This stubborn disinclination to leave the slum despite its obvious disadvantages is evident in Sillitoe's early fiction as well. The reader will recall that Harold Seaton in *Key to the Door* 'clung to the town centre because its burrow was familiar and comfortable', and that his wife Vera 'missed the sound of factory engines and traffic' on a visit to the country. Their sons Arthur and Fred find comfort in 'the maze of streets sleeping between tobacco factory and bicycle factory [which] drew them into . . . [its] bosom and embraced them in sympathetic darkness' (SNSM: 113). And those who are forced to leave, usually because of wartime conscription, find the urge to return home is overwhelming. Examples include Arthur Seaton's cousins, sons of Ada Doddoe, who desert time after time to return home; Donnie Hodson in 'To Be Collected', who follows a similar pattern; and Robert the Welshman in 'The Good Women', who finds shelter and warmth in the home of Liza Atkin.

As Jackson makes clear, working-class lack of mobility is based on other factors besides a preference for the familiar, however strong that may be. To begin with, there is little encouragement for formal education, or for informal education either if it comes from books. A number of sociologists echo T. R. Fyvel's observation in *The Insecure Offenders* that 'the majority of working-class boys and girls . . . [leave] school hardly educated at fifteen.' In the words of R. H. Tawney in *Equality*, 'working-class children . . . go to the mill at an age when the children of the well-to-do are just beginning the serious business of education.' The result, both in life and in Sillitoe's fiction, is usually what Ferdynand Zweig calls in *The British Worker* 'a blind-alley job'. Despite a widespread awareness of the outcome of early school leaving, Zweig notes that 'nearly all . . . [working-class adolescents] prefer working to being at school.' George Orwell states the case more forcefully: 'there is not one working-class boy in a thousand who does not pine for the day when he will leave school. He wants to be doing real work, not wasting his time on ridiculous rubbish like history and geography. To the working-class, the notion of staying at school till you are nearly grown-up seems merely contemptible and unmanly.' Echoes of this rejection of formal education are found throughout Sillitoe's Nottingham fiction, and the conviction that the proper place for adolescents of fourteen or fifteen is in a factory or shop rather than the classroom is widely held by his workers. The illustrations already set down in Chapter Four make the correspondence between art and life in this instance abundantly clear.

A concomitant, long-standing working-class attitude to education has been the discouragement of serious reading. Robert Roberts records its presence in Salford, a working-class district of Manchester, in the first quarter of the century: 'reading of any kind was often considered a frivolous occupation. "Put that book down!" a mother would command her child, even in his free time, "and do something useful."' In a *TLS* essay (October 15, 1971) entitled 'Class and the Novel' Melvyn Bragg points out that 'for a working-class household [in the forties and fifties] "books" were women's magazines or school prizes; a library was the place they opened on Tuesdays at the Friends' Meeting House, and the classics were illustrated paperbacks [comics] from Woolworths.' As recently as 1959, a year after the publication of *Saturday Night and Sunday Morning*, Richard Hoggart remarked that working-class reading was essentially limited to 'the Sunday gossip-with-sensation papers' such as the *News of the World* and the *Daily Mirror*. Sillitoe's readers will recall finding evidence of similar attitudes about reading in his work. In the Seaton family reading the *Daily Mirror* is an acknowledged part of weekend life, but Brian Seaton is made to feel intense guilt when he spends precious pennies that might have been used for food on *The Count of Monte Cristo* and Hugo's *Les Misérables*. Elsewhere in the early fiction the presence of books acts as a disruptive element in family life. There is, for example, the rage of Kathy, the wife of the narrator in 'The Fishing Boat Picture', when her husband Harry prefers reading to more physical activity, and the bewilderment and frustration of Jim Scarfedale when his wife Phyllis upbraids his complacency after she had read communist tracts about workers' rights. In the first instance it will be remembered that Kathy, who 'hated ... [books] like poison', heaped constant abuse on Harry's reading habit (LLDR: 82). In the second, Jim saw trouble brewing as soon as Phyllis 'started to read books all day' (LLDR: 150). In each case the marriage is destroyed.

It is to be expected that after leaving school, working-class adolescents will move into jobs requiring physical ability rather than intellectual training. It is likely that such jobs will be repetitive and unstimulating, and will soon becoming boring and tedious for those who hold them. There will also be little opportunity for advancement in most cases, and even should an opportunity occur, it is probable that the worker's lack of training in making critical and disciplined judgements would seriously limit his chance of success. As Raymond Williams points out in *Culture and Society 1780–1950*, it is a rare instance when 'anyone born into the industrial working-class escapes his function of replacement.' In other words, factory workers are seen simply as expendable accessories to the machinery of production, with one replacing another as a new machine part replaces one which has been broken or worn out. The social contract that defines this unenviable position is expressed succinctly by R. H. Tawney: 'the wage-earners act under ... [the plant owners'] direction; have access to the equipment, plant and machinery, without which they cannot support themselves, on condition of complying with the rules laid down, subject to the intervention of the State and of trade unions, by their employers; and work – and not infrequently live – under conditions which ... the latter have determined.' Lewis Mumford, in a bitter denunciation of this situation entitled 'The Insensate Industrial Town' (in *The Culture of Cities*), argues that during the depression 'the ruling classes wished to preserve individual initiative and freedom of contract (that is, social helplessness) for the workers: their right to accept starvation wages was held sacred.' Sillitoe's derisive echo of this, found in *Key to the Door* and noted earlier, is worth repeating here: 'Wage rates at Robinson's [factory] had been carefully regulated – set at a fraction above the dole money, enough to give the incentive of a regular job, but hardly enough to keep its employees far from a harrowing experience in near starvation.'

Even in better times, as Brian Jackson suggests, 'the working-class family has few, if any, financial assets. The man has nothing to live from except his labour and his skill. His job is unlikely ever to give him enough money to build up capital.... His earnings probably reach their peak in his early twenties, and thereafter ... [in normal times] they will hold still, or decline.' Young and Willmott make the same point. As a result, according to Hoggart, there is usually 'little room for manoeuvre financially [in the worker's family], only just enough to "wag on"; the housekeeping money is usually "mortgaged" to a penny or so and "scraping" is considered normal.' The same point is made by Madeline Kerr: 'however large the income, saving is impossible and everyone is broke by the end of the week.' And Norman Dennis in *Coal is Our Life* substantiates the total dependence on each week's wages when he says: 'the rhythm of domestic life is the rhythm of the working-day, the working-week, and the weekly wage-packet.' In an eloquent exposition of the worker's dilemma, Brian Jackson explains that with children working and living at home the family experiences a temporary but

> uncharacteristic prosperity.... It passes, and once the children leave home there begins the slow drop into the poverty band again. In middle age the risks of illness and accident increase, and without capital there are fewer cushioning devices to help the working-class couple. Finally retirement ... means the sharp and final drop to subsistence level.... This deep and terrible rhythm is the very ground of working-class life. It works its less visible course even in the more prosperous present. It reminds the man that his family lives by his physical strength, and that in a narrow way not felt by the rest of society, his wage-earning burns up his physical body. No one in our society has a shorter life than he.

Sillitoe's indictment of society for the wrongs he feels it has visited on working-class men and women finds ringing endorsement in Jackson's dispassionate assessment.

The financial precariousness of many working-class families is one factor in a widespread resentment of what J. B. Priestley and Ferdynand Zweig have called 'the boss class'.[3] Not only do the workers think of capitalist factory-owners as self-serving, selfish and greedy, according to Zweig, but they also harbour a deeply rooted indignation against the cavalier treatment so frequently meted out to them. They object, as Tawney points out, to the unfairness of property-owners being 'paid compensation for disturbance [while] workmen . . . [are] dismissed without appeal on the word of a foreman.' An awareness of this particular example of injustice is expressed by a number of Sillitoe's characters, and is echoed as well in Roberts' study of Salford. Orwell and Jackson cite other specific instances of injustice in the factory, and in Sillitoe's fiction (especially in *Saturday Night and Sunday Morning*, *Key to the Door* and 'The Good Women') there is a general and vigorous condemnation of industrial employers and their lack of consideration for the worker's position. The result of this, of 'no attempt . . . being made to fix a man's allegiance to the firm, or to consult his opinions and needs in any respect', is the formation of a strong sense of community among the workers from which owners and other managerial staff are excluded. Jackson and Dennis both note the 'severely defined upper limit' of this community, pointing out that even foremen are considered outsiders. The point is underscored in *Saturday Night and Sunday Morning* when Arthur Seaton describes his weekly encounter with Robboe, the bicycle factory foreman, as 'a time when different species met beneath white flags, with wage-packets as mediators.'

To understand more fully why 'the old antagonism of management and worker lives on', it is necessary to look at the self-image held by the majority of British working-class men. Michael Young in *The Rise of the Meritocracy 1870–2033* defines this self-image as 'the mythos of muscularity', an attitude of mind characterised by intense pride in physical labour and the presumption that the rest of society is dependent on that labour for its very existence. A number of sociological studies document the pervasiveness of this view. Zweig's research for *The British Worker* led him to the conclusion that 'many, if not most, workers have a romantic idea of the role and functions of their classes. The working-class is the backbone of the country, the most hard-working and the most useful class. . . . It gives the community more than it takes from it.' Dennis points to the working man's 'pride in being a worker, and his solidarity with other workers is a pride in the fact that they are real men who work hard for their living, and without whom nothing in society could function.' Many of Sillitoe's characters share this outlook. Ernie in 'The Other John Peel' is a typical working-class spokesman as he reminds his mate Bob that 'we wok in a factory, don't we? Well, we're the backbone of the country' (RD: 42). He goes on to argue that 'there's too many people on our backs and it's about time they was slung off' (RD: 42). The narrator in 'The Bike' is also convinced 'that rough work . . . [is] best' and he dreams about 'the workers taking over everything (like Dad wants to)' (RD: 105). Arthur and Brian Seaton, the Hodson brothers in 'To Be Collected', the strike inciter and Liza Atkin in 'The Good Women' subscribe to similar viewpoints. Each of them holds strongly to the fantasy of a re-organised society dominated by the workers, whom they feel have earned the right to run things through their apprenticeship to hard physical work.

While the central bias in working-class interpretations of social relationships – a distinction between *them* and *us* – is mentioned by most sociologists who examine British working-class life, their research reveals a number of variants in its application. Ferdynand Zweig points to a fundamental distinction between the two groups when he suggests that 'the average worker has only to look at a man to see whether he is one of them or not . . . when he sees strong horny hands, sometimes puffed up, and stained or greasy, he knows that he is one of "us". But if his hands are soft and obviously not used in his work, he belongs to the class of men... who are "they".' This finds its echo in Sillitoe's fiction when the narrator in 'The Bike' expresses his belief that during the Russian revolution 'they lined everybody up and made them hold their hands out and the working blokes went up and down looking at them. Anybody whose hands was lily-white was taken away and shot. The others was OK' (RD: 105). The narrator, who works in a factory himself, speculates that his labourer's hands would give him nothing to worry about should a similar situation arise in Britain as the result of a workers' revolution. The point here is that although the narrator is using a traditional working-class method of assessment in an exaggerated manner to suit his propagandistic purpose, it is nonetheless plausible in terms of real-life workers' image of themselves as men who contribute far more than they receive from society and to whom most forms of redress or retribution against 'those who bossed the world about' are justifiable (RD: 182).

The pervasiveness of a *them–us* habit of thought beyond the confines of factory walls may also be documented, perhaps most meaningfully in working-class attitudes towards *their* property. Richard Hoggart comments on the widely-held 'assumption that in public "anything goes".' He explains that in practice this means that 'people [are] ready to cheat in outside matters where in local matters they are normally honest.' There is a tradition of ' "seeing y' pals alright", which usually means cheating those outside, for whom you work, so as to show loyalty towards the group you know personally. You will not fiddle from your mate, but you will flog anything you safely can from the "firm" or the Services.' An explanation for this 'definitional disparity' in working-class thinking may be found in what Zweig in *Labour, Life and Poverty* calls 'a deeply-felt sense of injustice and grievance for what they regard as wrongs done to them in the past.' An opportunity to steal from *them*, therefore, is seen as a chance to 'get yer own back', as Hoggart points out. Evidence of the widespread acceptance of this attitude leads Brian Jackson to conclude that 'most working-class families ... have handled small amounts of stolen property all their lives' and David Downes to refer to the working-class 'institutionalisation of theft from institutions or the rich.' Jackson also reminds us of the working-class truism that 'everyone knows ... it's best not to say exactly where a suit length or a Christmas bird came from, since magistrates subscribe to a different code of right and wrong – especially with regard to property.'

These attitudes are passed on from one generation to another. As Downes has observed, although working-class parents may not encourage stealing from *them*, 'they do not teach their children not to steal. With no internalized prohibitions against stealing, the child has no guilt problems to cope with, and the only factor to be considered is that of risk and "trouble".' As might be expected, the incidence of arrests and convictions for working-class children and adolescents is high. According to Madeline Kerr, 'it is quite usual for one child [in a family] to be at an approved school', and in her study of a small number of working-class families in Liverpool's Ship Street she records that 'twelve of the boys below ... [eighteen] are in Borstal or some other approved school.' In many cases working-class parents feel that legal penalties meted out to their children are unfairly severe. Kerr records a mother's anger when her twelve-year-old son is sentenced to three years for stealing 'a bottle of lemonade and some bananas from a greengrocer's.' Elsewhere she tells of a boy named Tom who was put in prison for five or six months for stealing from gas meters before being sentenced to Borstal: 'his mother went to the Police Station and said she did not want Tom sent there.... The police told Mrs M. that the case would come up on a Thursday and she had better come to court to plead for him on that day. She did so. She found the case had been heard on the Wednesday, the day before. The police had told her the wrong day purposely. Tom was sent to Borstal for three years.'

The sense of injustice generated by such treatment results in widespread antipathy towards the police, not only among working-class parents, but in their children as well. John

Townsend speaks of working-class boys' 'mercurial anger at authority' in *The Young Devils: Experiences of a School-Teacher*, and recalls his problems coping with young teenagers who shouted 'Soppy Copper' when policemen came to the school to check up on them for 'the usual – petty thieving [from] gas-meters' and other sources. Fyvel makes a more general assessment when he points to 'a single-minded acceptance of a state of Cold War between . . . [large numbers of working-class adolescents] and the police which was startlingly uniform.' Such observations are particularly relevant to a study of Sillitoe's early fiction, for not only do they help to explain the anti-police invective indulged in by his characters, but they also serve to authenticate the attitudes held by a number of his protagonists. The vehement denunciation of *them* by Smith in 'The Loneliness of the Long-Distance Runner', for instance, is both explicable and plausible in the light of sociological research. Like the people of Ship Street, Sillitoe's characters occasionally utilise the police 'for reasons of private vengeance' (as did Mrs Bull in *Saturday Night and Sunday Morning*), but 'when the police represent order then every attempt is made to hoodwink them.' As Kerr makes clear, 'the police are generally regarded with suspicion and it is believed that they will frame you for something you haven't done and anyhow are natural enemies.'

Evidence of the law being applied to the detriment of working-class people provides further explanation of antipathy towards *them*. John M. Martin suggests in *Juvenile Vandalism, A Study of its Nature and Prevention* that 'the law-enforcement process works undue hardships on lower-class people. . . . For any offences they commit . . . [they] are more likely to be arrested, to be found guilty, and to be imprisoned than are their more affluent [and] prestigeful (sic) . . . counterparts.' The argument is reinforced by a statement made by Winston Churchill early in his parliamentary career. Presenting legislation during his first term as Home Secretary, he pointed to class discrimination in law enforcement: 'The House will, I think, support me in any steps that may be

necessary to prevent these undesirable commitments [to gaol].
The evil falls on the sons of the working-classes. The sons
of other classes commit many of the same offences in their
boisterous and exuberant spirits in their days at Oxford and
Cambridge, for which scores of the sons of the working
classes are committed to prison.'

A number of reputable sociologists, including Downes,
Fyvel, John Mays and B. M. Spinley, suggest that continuing
confrontation between *them* and *us* is unavoidable under
present conditions. In 1954 Mays concluded in *Growing Up
in the City* that England's working-class world is 'made up
of a number of inter-related problems which produce a
complex of disadvantages and difficulties that will remain for
a very long time to come to challenge the skill of the social
services of the "Welfare State".' Fyvel is more specific. In *The
Insecure Offenders* he points to deprivation experienced in the
fifties by working-class 'families and especially working-class
boys and girls dependent on public services. . . . It is they who
have suffered from . . . the shortage of trained probation
officers; from lack of playing-fields and sports facilities in
poorer areas and from niggardly public grants to youth
clubs; probably most of all from the shortage of school-
teachers, from overcrowded classes and the consequent lack
of individual attention.' Both Downes and Spinley record
the presence of a working-class code of aggressiveness which
Downes sees as 'a product in part of social factors – generations of low ascribed social status, poverty, unemployment
and overcrowding – in part of ecological factors – slum
streets, walled-in dockside or factory area milieu, lack of play
facilities, [and] deteriorating property.' Under such conditions Spinley has found a widespread acceptance of 'the
appropriateness of aggressive response' and in *The Deprived
and the Privileged* records a consequent 'attitude of rebellion
against [outside] authority.' Downes concludes: 'the encouragement of spontaneity and autonomy from an early age
leads the working-class boy to resist the assertions of middle-
class authority he is bound to encounter via school and the
law. Working-class culture is at once rigorously defined and

sufficiently at odds with the controlling middle-class culture to make a head-on clash almost inevitable.' In Sillitoe's stories these clashes take place so frequently that the reader who comes to them from an independent study of working-class life might be forgiven for reading them as made-to-order case histories of class confrontation. Throughout the early fiction Sillitoe presents a gallery of working-class aggressors who battle tirelessly against the middle-class world of *them*. From the youthful Smith to middle-aged Liza Atkin to ageing Harold Seaton, Sillitoe's private army of social dissidents engage in spiritual and physical combat against the forces of social oppression as they encounter them, the middle-class authority figures who 'tell you what to do ... use a different accent ... pay your wages, collect rent ... hand you the dole ... live on your backs ... tread you down.'

It is possible to document other meeting points of art and life in Sillitoe's work. It is at least equally interesting, though, to look briefly at two points where they diverge. While there is no essential disagreement between his portrayal and the consensus of researchers' conclusions about the physical conditions and basic attitudes which describe the British worker's position in society, there are two intriguing omissions in Sillitoe's picture. Both the dominant matriarchal figure of the working-class 'mum' and the working man's great passion, organised sport, are almost completely ignored in the Nottingham fiction. The significance of these particular omissions becomes clear only when one recalls Sillitoe's espousal of the novelist's role as social reformer. As Chapter Three shows, Sillitoe's conception of the novelist's function when he was involved in writing the early fiction depended on two basic assumptions: first, that the writer has a duty to concern himself with themes which reflect social injustice, and second, that he must continually remind his readers of the pressing need for reform.

Bearing this in mind, it is evident that Sillitoe excludes the decisive, influential 'mum' recorded in most studies of working-class life because her presence would blunt the reformist thrust of his art. To begin with, the 'mum' figure represents tradition, according to Young and Willmott: 'they hold to . . . the old ways more tenaciously than other members of the family.' Sillitoe's men, on the other hand, spend much of their energy in the early fiction in confrontation with tradition, denouncing traditional attitudes and actions which they feel cause unfair treatment and wreak unnecessary hardship on members of the working-class. Then there is what Hoggart calls 'the myopic nature of the lives of most working-class mothers . . . it can produce a turned-in-upon-itself world into which nothing which does not concern the family penetrates.' Yet to make an effective criticism of larger concerns, such as the worker's position in society, it is imperative that the writer's spokesmen observe and experience a wider spectrum of social interaction. For this reason Sillitoe prefers to focus on his male characters, who can be expected to have a range of practical experience unavailable to the average 'mum'. It is also arguable that Sillitoe is unwilling to emphasise the leadership qualities ascribed to the typical 'mum' because in so doing he might somehow dilute the characterisation of his men as forceful spokesmen in the fight for social justice. (A curious footnote to this discussion is found in the assertion of Norman Dennis that only in reference to their mothers can working-class men 'speak of love without embarrassment.' It is artistically fitting, then, that in the Nottingham fiction there is no 'mum' who calls forth such speech from Sillitoe's men. Their signature is anger, and that is surely a more appropriate emotion to sustain them in their continuing battle against the victimising world of *them*.)

The reader of Sillitoe's early work who is also familiar with working-class life will no doubt be aware of his failure to devote more space to one of the more prominent features of that life, a passionate concern with organised sport. Occasional references to 'doing the pools' (predicting the outcome of football games) are found scattered through the Nottingham novels and stories. There is even one story entitled 'The Match', but the game in the story is only a means of focusing on the disturbed emotional state of the main character. That Sillitoe's characters do not concern themselves with organised sport is understandable when one realises how totally absorbing such an interest can be in real life. George Orwell's recollection of an experience 'in Yorkshire when Hitler invaded the Rhineland' is a case in point: 'Hitler, Locarno, Fascism and the threat of war aroused hardly a flicker of interest locally, but the decision of the Football Association to stop publishing their fixtures in advance ... flung all Yorkshire into a storm of fury.' Sillitoe wishes to direct the fury of his militant workers at other targets; he is unwilling to have them vitiate their anger on what are for him less significant issues. J. B. Priestley, in his celebrated novel *The Good Companions*, describes working men reacting to a football match: 'watching a ball shape Iliads and Odysseys for you ... turned you into a member of a new community, all brothers together for an hour and a half, for not only had you escaped from the clanking machinery of this lesser life, from work, wages, rent, doles, sick pay, insurance cards, nagging wives, ailing children, bad bosses, idle workmen, but you had escaped with most of your mates and your neighbours.' Sillitoe, on the other hand, wants his workers to belong to only one community bound together by a shared awareness of victimisation by *them*. Hoggart remarks on working-class admiration of certain prominent qualities in sports heroes, 'the exhibition of strength and muscle, of speed and daring, of skill and cunning,' and sees them as 'very modified modern counterparts of the heroes of saga, who combined natural physical gifts with great application and cunning in the use of them'. The reader may recall that these are the same qualities Sillitoe ascribes to his worker-heroes, with the significant difference that in his fiction these faculties are applied to criticism of and confrontation with representatives of an inequitable social system. It is significant that in 'The Loneliness of the Long-Distance Runner' Smith uses his talents to thwart *them* instead of to gain personal glory, and that he develops into a vociferous advocate of working-class grievances against the middle-class establishment, not into a track star.

While it is clear that Sillitoe's picture of working-class

life in Britain from about 1930 to 1960 is not fully comprehensive, it is also clear that his omissions are deliberate. Exercising the artist's right to select and reject from the raw material at hand, he has chosen to focus on those aspects of working-class life that might generate in his readers a recognition of the need for social reform, and to exclude any material that might undermine that response. Nonetheless there is abundant evidence to show that his representation is essentially accurate, and that his work has, in Brian Jackson's words, 'illustrated social truths in memorable ways.' Some readers may wish to argue that Sillitoe has paid too little attention to improvements in working-class standards of living between the depression years of the thirties and the decade following the war. But as G. D. H. Cole and Raymond Postgate conclude in *The Common People 1746–1946*, despite the gradual amelioration of conditions since the time of the Chartists, 'two nations [the working-class and the rest of society] still confronted each other in 1946.' And Brian Jackson, in the conclusion to his study twenty years later, remarks that the larger issue of persistent disparity between 'the two nations' is what really continues to matter. It is claimed, he says, that

> the working class is now changing so rapidly that the concerns advanced in this book are of historical interest only. There have always been people who felt this. At any point over the last hundred years it was felt that an old working class style of life was just disappearing: the English novel through Scott, Mrs Gaskell, Dickens, George Eliot, Hardy, Lawrence, records with wonderful delicacy exactly such an impression in almost every decade. The truth is that working-class life has always been changing, but also that the relative economic position of that class has altered little. At certain times it may be poorer or richer, but it is always the base of the pyramid.

Alan Sillitoe's accurate rendering of life at 'the base of the pyramid' in his Nottingham fiction not only offers us an insight into problems of legitimate social concern, but also provides us with a credible explanation for the intensity and conviction of reformist attitudes found here and in the first two novels of his trilogy.

Notes and References

[1] *The English Provinces c. 1760–1900: A Study in Influence.* Read refers here to 'England north of the Trent', which would include Nottingham.
[2] Evidence that large numbers of these houses remained occupied even in the sixties is not limited to Sillitoe's fiction. Norman Dennis estimated in *Coal is Our Life: An Analysis of a Yorkshire Mining Community* that in 1959 fully thirty per cent of the population of one Yorkshire town lived in 'back to backs'. Others, including T. R. Fyvel in *The Insecure Offenders* (1961), Hoggart and Kerr, pointed to a continuing shortage of adequate low-cost rental housing and its harsh consequences for working-class families. The author of this study visited Nottingham in April, 1978, to find a number of houses still occupied in the condemned streets of Old Radford despite long-standing Corporation promises of better accommodation.
[3] See John Braine, 'Lunch with J. B. Priestley,' *Encounter*, June 1958.

Chapter Seven

The Immediate Critical Response:

Reviewers' Reactions to the Early Fiction

The earliest reviews of Sillitoe's first novel, *Saturday Night and Sunday Morning*, appeared in the British Sunday papers on October 12, 1958. Like most first novels, it attracted little immediate critical attention, though John Wain in his review for the *Observer* recognised its importance as a statement about working-class life, and Richard Mayne in the *Sunday Times* caught something of its political significance. Within the week its presence had been recorded by five of the dailies, including the nationally-distributed *Daily Telegraph*, and by the respectable weekly *New Statesman*. Within the month it was examined briefly in the *Manchester Guardian*, where it had to compete for space with new work by Brendan Behan, Lawrence Durrell, Graham Greene and Iris Murdoch, and in the *Times Literary Supplement* (hereafter referred to as *TLS*), where it was one of three novels reviewed together. By the end of the year the *Observer* has listed it as one of the outstanding books of 1958, and on January 4, 1959, *Books and Bookmen* called it the best first novel of the previous year. Publication of *Saturday Night and Sunday Morning* in the United States in August, 1959, resulted in a number of serious reviews, including perceptive commentaries by Irving Howe and Anthony West. It was West, writing in the *New Yorker*, who made the most memorable statement about Sillitoe's achievement: 'Even if he never writes anything more, he has assured himself a place in the history of the English novel.'[1]

West's assertion rests on his argument that the novel 'breaks new ground.' Like other reviewers, he realised that Sillitoe was not the first to write about working-class life. But West saw him as the first to treat that life in coherent detail 'as a normal aspect of the human condition.' He argued that earlier writers had been unable to capture either working-class values or the working-class point of view accurately. Either such writers 'in the process of acquiring the ambition to write and learning how to do it [had] lost touch with their origins and unconsciously acquired the outlook and the values of the middle class, or they were ... good, honest bourgeois projecting themselves downward in the social scale for the good of their guilt-ridden souls.' He pointed to George Owell as an example of the well-meaning writer about the working-class who, try as he might, could never be 'on the inside looking in', as Sillitoe was. In *Saturday Night and Sunday Morning*, on the other hand, West felt that not only was working-class life being used as 'natural subject matter for a writer' for the first time, but that it was finally being 'written by someone who understands it and its values.'

This new angle of vision, so important to West's assessment, also excited other reviewers. The idea of an authentic worm's eye view of society figures in the reactions of a number of them to Sillitoe's novel. The Nottingham papers might have been expected to praise the achievement of a native son – and they did – but they would also be among the first to detect falseness in his portrayal of local working-class conditions. Yet not only do they make mention of recognisable geography in the city's working-class areas, but they also point to the novel's accurate representation of local working-class dialect and attitudes, as well as to the author's personal and intimate experience of the life he explores in the novel. More important, however, is the *Guardian Journal*'s suggestion that 'Mr Sillitoe has successfully captured a whole class, the working-class of Britain in the post-war era', a sentiment echoed in the *Nottingham Evening Post*: 'the story ...

might be told of a large section of the workers in any city anywhere in Britain.' In other words, while the picture of Nottingham working-class life was recognisable in its particulars, it was also seen to be representative of British working-class life in general. Roy Perrott, making this point in the *Manchester Guardian*, felt that Sillitoe's novel has 'a glow about it as though he had plugged in to some basic source of the working-class spirit.' Richard Mayne in the *Sunday Times* made a similar point when he wrote of the authentic idiom of this 'unassuming but very outspoken and vivid glimpse of working-class life.' Perhaps the most quotable assessment was made by Peter Green in the *Daily Telegraph: 'Saturday Night and Sunday Morning* is that rarest of all finds: a genuine, no-punches-pulled, unromanticised working-class novel, which makes *Room at the Top* look like a vicarage tea-party by comparison.' In subsequent advertising Sillitoe's publishers, W. H. Allen, made much use of Green's statement. Maurice Richardson said in his review for the *New Statesman* that the novel 'makes an immediate impression of being very much the real thing.' His assessment was echoed by John Wain in the *Observer*: 'I know nothing about the interior life of a typical lathe operator, and not very much about his exterior life; but I felt confident, reading Mr Sillitoe's book, that I was getting a truthful account. It felt solid and accurate.' This quality of verisimilitude was also evident to American reviewers. James Yaffe in the *Saturday Review* called it 'the honesty and authenticity of his writing – the fact that when he describes an English working-class home, we feel sure that we are seeing the real thing, not a sentimental Hollywood substitute.'

Moreover, perceptive reviewers were aware that the strength of *Saturday Night and Sunday Morning* was not wholly defined by its author's 'virtuoso ability to describe the sight, sound and smell' of working-class life. As Malcolm Bradbury pointed out in the *New York Times Book Review*, 'Alan Sillitoe ... has caught much of the mood of the present-day working-class in England – its half-conscious spirit of rebellion, its exploitive laziness and non-co-operation, its uneasy respect for law and order, its secret sympathy for the clever rogue and the army deserter, its sense of a distant, vague "they" which runs its life so that you can never win.' Maurice Richardson remarked that 'what is so good about the book is [not only] the vividness of the detailed description of pub, factory and kitchen life, [but also] ... the statement of the working-class attitude of instinctive anarchism, of "it's all a racket", typified by those winks which you see the cynical toilers exchanging in factory and yard.' Reviewers on both sides of the Atlantic shared the opinion that the magnetic quality of *Saturday Night and Sunday Morning* lay largely in its ability to hold their 'attention by its evident truth to working-class psychology.' They were generally agreed with Malcolm Bradbury that the novel offered a view of life conditioned by a sense of personal oppression by 'the eternal "they", a vague conspiratorial entity' that perpetuated social inequity at the expense of the working class. John Wain summed up this attitude when he pointed out that 'all the characters, but particularly the hero, have the deep-rooted sense of being exploited, bamboozled, lied to and generally made use of by a nameless "they", the possessing, ruling class, who exist as a kind of faceless pin-striped army of puppet-masters, working away in a dimension where they can't be got at.' Other reviewers shared Wain's concern, seeing the reactions of Sillitoe's characters against real or imagined exploitation by *them* as the most important issue in the novel.

Many reviewers saw Arthur Seaton as a symbol of working-class protest against *them*. And while assessments of Arthur's activities and attitudes varied from one review to the next, as might be expected, there was nonetheless a remarkable correlation of opinion about his essential nature, both as an individual and as a representative of his class. Arthur was generally seen as a rebel, an anarchist reacting violently and desperately against the regimented society that kept him and his class marching in clearly defined tracks. He was most frequently described as a rogue, a term which indicates a certain sympathy for his position, incorporating as it does the feeling that his actions could be considered mischievous rather than reprehensible. Such a response indicates that at least some of Arthur's actions and attitudes were seen to be justified because of society's treatment of his class. Curiously, however, none of the contemporary reviewers was disturbed by an obvious conflict between Arthur's personal rebellion against the pressures of conformity and his role as a representative of more widespread working-class reaction against *them*. Though it is clear that aspects of Arthur's personal rebellion, such as his adultery with Brenda and Winnie, are morally indefensible, and that such actions clearly vitiate his position as a spokesman against the immorality of a society that treated his class unfairly, reviewers failed to explore the issue. Only the *TLS* approached the matter, obliquely, when it pointed out that Sillitoe seemed to be holding society to blame for all of Arthur's misdemeanours, thereby ignoring the principle of individual responsibility for one's actions. And Irving Howe, in a different context, criticised Sillitoe's abnegation of artistic responsibility by being 'remarkably indulgent' towards the actions of his protagonist.

Surprisingly, there was general agreement in the original reviews that at the end of *Saturday Night and Sunday Morning* Arthur Seaton ceases to rebel and accepts whatever rules society imposes on him. Anthony West, for example, says that when the book ends, Arthur 'is no longer the randy boozer looking for a bit of fun but a mature man looking for a decent future and in a fair way toward making himself one.' His comment is echoed by John Wain: 'Arthur's discontent is shown to be considerable but not intolerable; at the end he marries and settles down with a fair promise of something like contentment.' Such assumptions would seem to be as much the result of inattentive reading of the novel's final chapter as they are reflections of a middle-class pattern of wishful thinking that Sillitoe has forcefully rejected in his fiction. For it is perfectly clear in the final paragraphs of the novel that Arthur will continue to rebel, both as an individual and as a member of his class. The novel's concluding sentences, which describe Arthur's rebellious thoughts and symbolic combat with the fish he has just hooked, clearly reaffirm the belligerent protest that has shaped his previous life. It would seem, then, that while the reviewers of *Saturday Night and Sunday Morning* were willing to point out Sillitoe's indictment of society and to comment on his picture of working-class conditions (what Roy Perrott called the vitality of his social realism), they were not yet willing to entertain his conclusions about the inevitability of continuing social strife.

Their brief criticisms of Sillitoe's technical competence ranged from incisive comment to cliché. Most of them were impressed by his telling use of sensual detail to recreate the working-class environment of home, factory and pub. Gene Baro, for example, referred in the *New York Herald Tribune Book Review* to the novel's aural stimuli: 'one hears the slap of the machine belts, the raised voices of neighbourhood arguments, the drunken singing just before closing time.' And Peter Green in his review spoke of Sillitoe as a 'writer who knows his milieu and describes it with vivid, loving precision – the cramped family life, the generosity to children, the smell of suds and shaved metal at a work-bench, the violent, unformulated longings.' Some reviewers were concerned about the seeming haphazard arrangement of this 'exhaustive detail' into a coherent structural pattern. John Wain pointed out that while 'there is plenty of action, both amatory and violent', the novel had 'no real "plot".' Irving Howe put it another way: 'essentially the novel is a series of vignettes, like a succession of movie stills without much continuity or climax. Its faint pretence of a plot rests on little more than Arthur's final decision to drop his wild-catting and accept the restraints of domesticity.' One is tempted to point out in Sillitoe's defence that it is a rare first novel that is not flawed in some fashion; still, there can be little argument with these assessments of artistic weakness in *Saturday Night and Sunday Morning*. However, the vitality of the work and the fact that it was a first novel served to minimise commentary on Sillitoe's craftsmanship. Only two reviewers attempted to explore the crucial relationship between the author and his protagonist; and they came to opposing conclusions. Though there was agreement that Sillitoe was 'writing not about a displaced intellectual but a genuine working man', James Yaffe felt that the author made Arthur 'much too conscious of his unselfconsciousness, too aware, in a literary way, of what a vigorous young animal he is.' He argued that we are always seeing Arthur from the outside, from the author's point of view. Gene Baro took a different view. For him, the novel 'gains in force [precisely] because so much of what is thought or said belongs to Arthur's consciousness.' There is, of course, a measure of truth on both sides. There can be little doubt about Sillitoe's lack of detachment from his hero, for it is particularly evident in his continued failure to condemn any of Arthur's actions. Yet his characterisation of Arthur is forceful, consistent and credible. Set against the heroes of Sillitoe's later work Arthur stands out, independent and idiosyncratic, as a memorable and original creation.

Sillitoe's next work, the collection of short stories entitled *The Loneliness of the Long-Distance Runner*, was first reviewed in Lord Beaverbrook's *Sunday Express* on September 20, 1959. It soon became a bestseller, helped by the generally laudatory reviews and no doubt by the publicity of the publisher, who persisted in advertising it as a 'novel'. Once again reviewers praised the book's verisimilitude. John Berrie, in a review for the *Nottingham Evening Post*, made a point of mentioning the book's 'authenticity' of setting; and Roy Perrott in the *Guardian* took note of the language, 'whose tone and pitch Sillitoe has once again caught perfectly.' John Coleman, writing for the *Spectator*, found that 'the "feel" of the background seems right every time', and Pamela Hansford Johnson in the *New Statesman* agreed. Asserting that working-class fiction deals with 'a section of society which has to be known at first hand to be understood' and that 'all the imaginative sympathy in the world can't fake this kind of thing', Miss Johnson revealed that she had 'felt a sense of absolute trust' in the credibility of Sillitoe's fictional world as she read the stories in the collection.

As earlier chapters of this study have shown, the world of Britain's working-class has its own set of social imperatives. To reviewers who took the time to examine affinities among the various stories in *The Loneliness of the Long-Distance Runner*, this special ethos was readily apparent. Graham Hough in the *Listener* saw Sillitoe's characters collectively as 'the cramped, the poor, the dispossessed', and pointed out that these stories 'suggest how many of them there [still] are behind the façade of the welfare state.' R. G. G. Price, writing for *Punch*, said that Sillitoe's fictional world was defined by 'life stunted, not life triumphant.' Gene Baro in the *New York Herald Tribune Book Review* came closer to the mark when he spoke of Sillitoe's stories emphasising 'the spiritual isolation of the British working class from the larger body of British society'. 'The "class war",' he noted, 'is seen in its moral, but fundamentally non-political, manifestations.' Dramatic evidence of this working-class opposition to the conventional social ethics of other classes was revealed in John Updike's review for the *New Republic*. Entitled 'Voices From Downtroddendom', it spoke of the collection's title story as an inversion of the well-established genre of English schoolboy literature. In this genre the young hero, stimulated by a vision of glory for school or nation, exhibits the middle and upper class 'social virtues of endeavour, pluck and fair play' and wins the day, 'kicking the winning goal', just when all seems lost. In *The Loneliness of the Long-Distance Runner*, however, the working-class adolescent is not boarding at 'Eton or Willows-in-the-Dale but [is incarcerated in] an Essex Borstal.' He 'makes his mighty effort not to win the race but to lose it; [and] the nation for whom he strives is not Green England but the black kingdom of Downtroddendom.' The 'spiritual isolation of the working-class' is also noted in *Time's* review, which begins by quoting a relevant passage from Disraeli's *Sybil*: ' "I was told", continued Egremont, "that an impassable gulf divided the Rich from the Poor; I was told that the Privileged and the People formed Two Nations, governed by different laws, influenced by different manners, with no thoughts or sympathies in common." ' The anonymous reviewer, echoing the conclusions about continuing class divisions made by G. D. H. Cole and Raymond Postgate in 1946, saw evidence in Sillitoe's stories that 'the two nations still eye each other across a gulf nearly as impassable' as it was in Disraeli's time. He concluded on a more positive note, suggesting that in Sillitoe 'the largely silent second nation had found a brilliantly articulate spokesman.' Other reviews were marked by an awareness of what David Boroff in *Saturday Review* called 'the mystique of class warfare.' *The Times*, for example, spoke of 'the calm and dedicated campaign [against the rest of society] urged by Mr Sillitoe's characters', and concluded that the stories resembled 'a war correspondent's reports from some fantastic front which although it is all around us, is only sometimes visible.'

For the many reviewers who focused their attention on Smith, the aggressive protagonist of the title story, the battleground should have been clearly visible. Most of them, however, chose to see Smith as a victim of his background rather than as a champion of working-class grievances. This is not to say that his belligerent stance towards *them* was ignored by the critics. Muriel Spark in the *Observer* referred to his 'choking resentments' of *their* treatment of his class, and Pamela Hansford Johnson showed the depth of his feeling when she wrote: 'To defy Them means Borstal, clink, the rope – all right: with the pride of hate, he accepts the lot.' But by and large reviewers saw Smith as an unhappy example of social deviance from some undefined, presumably middle-class, standard of behaviour. John Coleman called the story 'a remarkable essay in delinquency . . . [which tells us a great deal] about the mentality of the incorrigible outlaw.' R. G. G. Price spoke of 'this wonderful glimpse into the criminal mind'; and Malcolm Bradbury in the *New York Times Book Review* said the story was 'a major study in [personal] rebellion.' *The Times* had pointed out that the book did 'not invite discussion in purely literary terms', and the implication in some reviews was that Sillitoe meant *The Loneliness of the Long-Distance Runner* to be read as an object lesson in the psychology of a delinquent, and that a close study of it could result in improved understanding and treatment of juvenile offenders. Pointing to Smith's rebellion against authority, Penelope Mortimer in the *Bookman* said that Sillitoe speaks 'clearly and calmly of what he knows – and what we should make it our business to find out.' Dee Wells, in her review for the *Sunday Express*, was more explicit. Beginning rather melodramatically – 'tomorrow a lonely boy named Smith will come into the life of anybody who cares about the future of Britain' – she argued that Smith was important 'because information about him – and about all the boys like him – if properly digested, could be of use to every interested person in the country from Rab Butler down through prison officers, probation officers, parsons, and schoolteachers, to the youngest cop on the beat.'

Whether or not Smith was to be seen as an aggrieved spokesman for his class or as a victim of it, there were a number of critics who found him unconvincing. The *TLS* reviewer suggested that 'the "honesty" and the depth of the rejection here carry no conviction'; and Muriel Spark felt that Smith's 'motives are never made clear enough.' As a result, the reader has to contend with what Anthony West in the *New Yorker* called Sillitoe's 'unabashed presence' in the work. Two questions were raised by those reviewers who were unhappy about Sillitoe's authorial intrusions. First, there was a feeling that Sillitoe was giving his character a sense of logic and intellectual grasp well beyond his years and experience. As John Updike put it, 'one is led to wonder if a sense of alienation as logical and systematic as Smith's is not so exceptional as to be unreal.' Second, there was a reluctance to accept as genuine Smith's command of language. According to the *TLS*, Sillitoe realised that 'the rejection of society by a sixteen year old is not sufficiently convincing when amplified in his own colloquial prose' and tried to 'jazz it up' with language inappropriate to his semi-articulate hero. The result, it argued, is that when Smith 'scrawls an especially eloquent phrase with the stub of the pencil he purports to be holding we can hear Mr Sillitoe breathing down his neck.' One does not have to look very hard at the story to find justification for such criticism, but as Graham Hough explained, 'Sillitoe's characters seem obliged occasionally to step outside themselves, to become more literate and analytical than they should, in order to make their points.' In other words, Sillitoe's zeal as a social crusader was threatening to overtake his craftsmanship, causing him at times to blur the distinction between author and hero. Perceptive reviewers, conscious of the difficulties this could cause, were beginning to warn him of its consequences.

The other eight stories in the collection received much less attention than the commanding title story. Critical reaction was generally favourable to this 'vigorous and original set of sketches', with particular commendation given to what Pamela Hansford Johnson called Sillitoe's 'literary tact and . . . sense of design.' Gene Baro, for example, said that 'a virtue of Mr Sillitoe's stories is . . . that all is achieved simply, matter-of-factly, without apparent striving for effect.' And the *London Magazine* reviewer pointed out that 'technique throughout . . . is triumphantly unobtrusive. The story called "The Fishing Boat Picture" is a shining example of the maximum effect produced by the minimum of apparent design.' Other critics were beginning to notice Sillitoe's penchant for sardonic humour. John Updike mentioned the 'rasp' and 'comedy' coupled with 'a casually callous acceptance of misery'; Roy Perrott pointed to 'the tragi-comic element' in stories such as 'The Fishing Boat Picture' and 'The Disgrace of Jim Scarfedale'; and Gene Baro spoke ambiguously about Sillitoe's 'robust and yet . . . restrained sense of the comic.' There was some dissenting opinion on the effectiveness of individual stories, and criticism of Sillitoe's style, which was to colour evaluations of some of his later books, was beginning to be heard. John Updike was unhappy with the language in 'Uncle Ernest', which he found 'not always appropriate to the subject', and he felt that the central incident in 'Noah's Ark', Colin's ride on the roundabout, was 'smothered under aloof phrase-making.' John Coleman commented that Sillitoe had a 'trick of unexpectedly flamboyant images that blaze out of a laconic page, sometimes embarrassingly, but once or twice (as at the end of 'The Fishing Boat Picture') with a peculiar and quite original effectiveness.' And the *TLS* reviewer argued with some justification that 'The Match' is 'pitched off-balance by the last line which turns what might have been a near perfect re-creation of a bit of life into a [melo-] drama.' On balance, though, the reviewers treated *The Loneliness of the Long-Distance Runner* well. They continued to pay attention to Sillitoe's social message, as they had in *Saturday Night and Sunday Morning*, and to see his use of working-class perspectives as a source of originality and strength. Although there were qualifications about his technical competence in some of the stories, the majority of critics seemed to agree that he had created 'a minor masterpiece' in the title story. Malcolm Bradbury captured the feeling of many of his colleagues when he concluded that 'Alan Sillitoe is certainly, on this showing, a major writer who ought to be read.'

Sillitoe's next novel of working-class life, *Key to the Door*, was published in October, 1961. In the meantime he had published *The General* (May, 1960). Although the most quoted review of that novel had been entitled 'Go Back to Nottingham, Mr Sillitoe', *Key to the Door* should not be considered a response to the reviewer's advice, for the new novel had been completed and was being revised when *The General* was released. Once again critics were drawn to Sillitoe's credible portrayal of the working-class milieu, even though this novel dealt primarily with an earlier period, the decade preceding the Second World War. Wayne Booth in the *Yale Review* found the picture convincing: 'this must have been the way it was, for Sillitoe, or for others just like him.' Frank Kermode in the *Partisan Review* pointed to Sillitoe's 'careful and elaborate reconstruction of the details of working-class life at the time', and concluded that 'nothing with this kind of accuracy could fail to have value.' George McMichael's review for the *San Francisco Sunday Chronicle* commended Sillitoe's convincing presentation of 'the agonising picturesqueness of slum life' as 'both a potent social indictment and an effective literary accomplishment.' Walter Allen in the *New York Times Book Review* and Arnold Kettle in the *Daily Worker* also praised the novel's verisimilitude. Kettle called it 'one of the most profound, imaginative pictures of working-class life in the thirties I have read'; and Allen said that the 'recreation of the industrial misery . . . the hopelessness, poverty and squalor of urban life at the time' was brilliant.

With the publication of *Key to the Door*, a growing number of critics were ready to agree with David Caute, who wrote in *Time and Tide* that Sillitoe stood 'in the forefront as describer and interpreter of working-class life, not only among contemporary writers, but within the whole English tradition.' Malcolm Bradbury qualified the assessment, however, when he said in *Punch* that Sillitoe was writing not of the working-class in general, but of 'the *lower* working-class, the tougher, less socialised, more rebellious segment among whom "pinching" is standard practice and society is seen as a racket, a stunt, a cheat.' Most reviewers were less willing to split hairs, however, and focused instead on the problems of life at subsistence level and the means of coping with them. Irving Howe pointed to the dependence on human, rather than material, resources evident in 'the dense affection and quarrelsome solidarity of the Seaton family life', and noted Sillitoe's 'profound conviction as to the dignity, warmth, and protective cohesion of working-class life.' William Barrett in the *Atlantic* referred to the resilience of Sillitoe's embattled characters in the face of difficulty: 'though living in slums and imprisoned by the dull routines of the factories, these people retain some unkillable earthy and peasant-like quality, a caged but not altogether crushed animal vitality.' Most reviewers discussed how this vitality, an integral part of what Howe called the 'communal spirit of the English worker', was frequently channelled into conflict with the representatives of other classes.

The catalyst for most expressions of working-class grievances in *Key to the Door* is the novel's protagonist, Brian Seaton. Because of his family's poverty, aggravated by his father's inability to find work, Brian spends much of his boyhood scavenging on municipal garbage tips for items of domestic and industrial waste which can be used or recycled and sold for grocery money. In the process, according to George McMichael, he 'develops the canniness of a beaten dog and a set of principles clearly in opposition to the standards of the "Establishment".' By the time he goes to work as a factory labourer at the age of fifteen and witnesses at first hand the exploitation of workers by wealthy factory owners, Brian has developed a fierce 'loyalty . . . to his class.' 'The cement of that loyalty,' according to Samuel Hynes in the *Commonweal*, 'is his sense of the need for solidarity against the whole of society above him.' David Caute saw Brian's militancy developing 'slowly, subconsciously, from a series of disconnected impressions, his out-of-work father wasting his life and beating his mother, the constant scratching for shillings, a traditional, almost cultural hatred of employers and their Conservative party, memories of Communist speakers, also working men, addressing crowds outside factories. . . . Brian's outlook is born of myth as well as reason.' According to Arnold Kettle, by the time Brian is conscripted for service in Malaya, where the government is fighting a running battle with Communist insurgents, he has learned 'a lot about cruelty and exploitation . . . and who his enemies are.' Taking part in what he clearly regards as an imperialist venture by *them*, Brian recognises the disconcerting irony of his position, 'that he is now a They', and he determines to do something about it. In David Caute's view, Brian realises the insanity of 'a young conscript, under military discipline and eight thousand miles from home', rebelling openly, yet 'he can, and does, go through with his personal protest.' When he is attacked by one of the insurgents, whom he regards as 'little blokes' oppressed by the same Establishment he opposes, Brian disarms his assailant and lets him go. A short time later, when his patrol is ambushed in the jungle, Brian deliberately directs his fire away from the Communist attackers. As the reviewer in *Time* concluded, 'all the conditioning of military training and

Mother England falls before the conditioning of Nottingham and Dad and the dole.'

Frank Kermode began his commentary on *Key to the Door* with a statement that 'class – how it conditions morality and even how it binds or dissolves national communities – continues to preoccupy English novelists; the more serious and ambitious they feel, the franker their expressions on this topic.' While the critic can only speculate on the degree to which Sillitoe's outspoken working-class bias in the early fiction reflected his desire to be taken seriously as a novelist, it is certain that most reviewers read his history of Brian Seaton as a social or a political statement about class. There were conflicting opinions about its significance, as might be expected, so that the novel was seen both as 'a potent social indictment' of an inequitable social structure and as a work 'in which social conscience plays an exacerbated part.' David Caute compared *Key to the Door* with *Saturday Night and Sunday Morning* and *The Loneliness of the Long-Distance Runner* and found in the latest work a more 'quiet, compassionate, controlled resentment at social injustice.' John Fuller in the *Listener* saw the novel representing a working-class rejection of manipulation by the political Establishment, made clear as Brian 'defies the rulers who kept his family on the dole before the war and used him to uphold imperialism after it.' Samuel Hynes also pointed to working-class conflict with a controlling élite, evident in Brian's zealous desire for 'freedom from poverty, from regimentation, and from the power of the governing classes.' John Coleman suggested in the *New Statesman* that what Sillitoe does 'is to make one aware as never before of the tough difference between a sympathetic "understanding" of what it has meant to be working-class and the blunt actuality in terms of parents-on-the-dole, pride under hand-outs, and sheer massive distrust of Them.' A similar sentiment informed Arnold Kettle's review: he concluded that *Key to the Door* was a 'political novel in the best and deepest sense – [because it is] a book that makes us see politics in individual terms and human beings in political terms.'

Other reviewers found the novel's social documentation less impressive. For example, Simon Raven in the *Spectator* saw Brian as 'little more than a convenient excuse for Mr Sillitoe to lecture us, exhaustively, on the vile conditions and mutilated psyches of the slums.' Cyril Connolly in the *Sunday Times* felt that Sillitoe's social statement was weaker here than it had been in earlier work: 'the rebel stance, so taut in *The Loneliness of the Long-Distance Runner*, has become a vague chip-on-the-shoulder near Communism.' Walter Allen found Brian's distrust 'of the behaviour and motives of all born outside his own class' to be 'insufficiently communicated.' He was also unhappy about the expression of Brian's 'left-wing sympathies' which he considered to be 'as puerile as they are vague.' And the *Library Journal*, which phrased its objections more delicately, warned that 'a little sex, a few four letter words ... and a certain exuberant sympathy for communism may disturb the cautious book selector.'

The 'insufficiently communicated' political statement in the novel leads to 'major damage', according to Irving Howe. As Howe reads the character of Brian Seaton, 'he is meant to be not merely an instinctive rebel, but a rebel searching for a rationale by which to live and act, so that his refusal to fire at the Communist guerillas comes to be "the key to the door", the act of defiance by which he discovers the meaning of his anger.' But Howe felt that Sillitoe failed 'to justify Seaton's concluding act.' He argued that 'nothing that has been shown to us, other than a few bare hints concerning Communist shop stewards in England, warrants the supposition that Seaton would refuse to shoot or would have any understanding as to why he refuses. More important, nothing in the novel indicates that Sillitoe has thought through the significance of the conclusion he provides.' Howe went on to suggest that 'Seaton does not refuse to shoot the guerillas because they are fellow human-beings; presumably, if they were of another political color, his hand would not tremble at the gun. ... A humanitarian or ethical justification for his conduct is thus ruled out, while a political one remains unprovided; all that is left, then, is a gratuitous and senti-mental gesture.'

Though Howe argues persuasively, he is not wholly con-vincing. What he fails to take into account is Brian's equa-tion of Malayan insurgents and Nottingham workers. Both groups, as Brian sees it, are carrying on a guerilla war against representatives of the same Establishment. Brian's refusal to kill the insurgent is a dramatic affirmation of this belief, and it has been carefully prepared for in Brian's life-long feeling of victimisation and exploitation by the representatives of entrenched privilege. Howe is right, though, that Sillitoe's attempt to give Brian's acts a political significance, by inject-ing references to communism at crucial moments, is con-fusing. It was evident to other reviewers as well that Sillitoe's strength did not lie in providing a coherent intellectual framework for the actions of his characters, at least in the early fiction. As George McMichael remarked, Sillitoe is at his weakest in *Key to the Door* when he tries to be 'philo-sophical and weighty.' Still, as David Caute pointed out, Brian's 'small act of revolution is at once both private in scope and public in implication.' Not only does it represent a personal satisfaction for Brian, but it also gives the reader at least an embryonic vision of the brotherhood and social justice that Sillitoe's workers continually seek.

Francis Hope, in the first review of Sillitoe's work to appear in *Encounter*, called *Key to the Door* 'a disappointing book', and one of his principal objections was to the author's style. According to Hope, 'when Mr Sillitoe tries to decorate his documentary, the metaphors tend to mix, the word–order stumbles, and the far-fetched adjectives pile up in a semantic long-jam.' The anonymous *TLS* reviewer disliked Sillitoe's 'rash of double-barrelled adjectives – "his too-choosing sight," "the brass–bed raft of sleep," "all-embracing fog-dragon of the night".' He (or she) went on to question the appropriateness of Sillitoe's metaphors, and in a memorable, though exaggerated, barb suggested that Sillitoe's use of ' "Ave yer mashed, mam?" becomes almost as wearisome a cliché as "Anyone for tennis?".' John Coleman was unhappy about the indulgent use of jargon, quoting the following passage to make his point: 'Born of a breaking-point, his loneliness was a brain-flash at the boundary of his early stress.' The objection made by Hans Koningsberger in the *Saturday Review* was more amusing but none the less damning, for Koningsberger was disturbed by 'a painfully poetic interlude of passion, in which we suddenly stumble over the announcement that the girl was "in her birthday suit".'

Other critics argued that Sillitoe had failed to provide a meaningful plot for his lengthy (446 page) novel. Francis Hope spoke of 'great slabs of raw material clumsily stacked together waiting for someone to make something of them.' Cyril Connolly pointed out that although 'there are some fine episodes . . . all traces of a master-hand or master policy are lacking. We leaf through an interminable album.' Hans Koningsberger felt that *Key to the Door* read 'like the pages of . . . any boy's diary', although he was willing to concede that at the moment of Brian's encounter with the guerilla 'all the diary entries point to a structure.' John Davenport in the *Observer* made a similar point. Calling the climactic scene one of 'the best things in the book', he nonetheless felt that it was 'a pity that this position was not reached sooner, as so many of the earlier pages could have been taken as read.' The critical objections were succinctly correlated by Wayne Booth, who remarked that the novel had 'no plot, little thematic coherence, no sequence to speak of . . . nothing but bare event'. Though Booth overstated the case, most critics shared the view that *Key to the Door* suffers from structural deficiencies. Sillitoe's candid recollection in the preface to a new edition of the novel in 1978, that 'the "form" of the book was not easy to organise', recognises critical opinion. On the other hand, his detailed account of the novel's long gestation period, growing from a report of the mountain climb written in 1949 to the pruning of three hundred pages from a late draft in 1960, and his careful explanation of the novel's thesis, show that he does not necessarily agree with it. On balance there is much to be said for Walter Allen's remarkably prescient conclusion that 'ambitious as it is, [*Key to the Door*] remains curiously tentative. It suggests that its author is still fumbling – though, remembering *Saturday Night and Sunday Morning* and *The Loneliness of the Long-Distance Runner*, it is difficult not to believe that before long he will be seen to have been fumbling to good purpose.'

The Ragman's Daughter, Sillitoe's second collection of stories about working-class life, was released in October, 1963, two years after publication of *Key to the Door*. For the most part reviewers were complimentary, though there was an unmistakable tone of *déja-vu* in many commentaries, coupled with suggestions that it was time for Sillitoe to explore new territory. As Mordecai Richler suggested in the *Spectator*, 'possibly the trouble is that *Saturday Night and Sunday Morning* was fresh, it had a certain purity, an enjoyment of the details of living that went beyond class, while the stories in *The Ragman's Daughter* seem the product of a shrewder writer reworking material he had already used.' According to Thomas Lask in the *New York Times*, the social message of the stories – that members of the working-class are 'beggars in time of depression, cannon fodder in time of war, but no one ever throws in the towel' in the fight with *them* – had already been well digested by the critics. David Storey wrote in the *Guardian* that Sillitoe's new stories 'back pedal over familiar ground' and 'make his revolutionary intentions the thing they should never be: charming.' And Karl Miller suggested in the *New Statesman* that Sillitoe's fiction was beginning to sound 'like something of a serial . . . the themes have something travelled, perfunctory about them now.' John Bowen, writing for the *New York Times Book Review*, used a striking image from *Key to the Door* to describe Sillitoe's position. Remembering the young Brian Seaton scouring the garbage dump for salvageable material to sell, he saw a similarity in Sillitoe 'raking over the experiences of his boyhood and adolescence in Nottingham. He rakes well. He has given us some gems – but each successive raking has found fewer of them, and more of what is obviously secondhand.' Bowen went on to suggest that 'whoever creates a [fictional] world . . . should tell us with each book more about the world. Mr Sillitoe tells us the same thing over and over again, and with each telling the values that inform the Seaton's world are seen to be less and less sufficient.' Both Bowen and Miller were particularly unhappy with the continuing emphasis in the new stories on the confrontation between *them* and *us*. Miller was bothered that in Sillitoe's work 'society is reduced to these two categories . . . those who belong to neither group . . . are nowhere.' And Bowen pointed out that 'human beings are not, in fact, so simply divided: we may deplore this, but we should accept it.' While there is certainly a point to be made here, that the writer does himself a disservice by oversimplifying social complexities, it should be pointed out that in Sillitoe's view (shared by many experienced sociologists) the working-class picture of society *is* a simplistic one. As he pointed out in the *Anarchy* article, 'the poor know of only two classes in society. Their sociology is much simplified. There are *them* and *us*.'

Although they felt that the social message had an all-too-familiar ring, most critics praised the technical competence exhibited in *The Ragman's Daughter*. The *Virginia Quarterly Review* commentator spoke well of Sillitoe's characterisation, pointing to 'sharply etched portraits of people of substance, passionate, tough, indestructible.' Julian Jebb in the *Sunday Times* applauded the representation of Liza Atkin in 'The Good Women', calling her 'a Nottingham Mother Courage.' Other reviewers referred to the effectiveness of individual stories. The *TLS* critic commended 'The Magic Box', 'about a marriage which goes wrong for reasons which are put before us with clarity and force.' P. N. Furbank spoke in *Encounter* of the story's emotional force, and Irving Wardle in the *Observer* suggested that 'Sillitoe's use of the radio, first as a lovingly described object and then as a metaphor uniting the complex elements of the narrator, is that of a master storyteller.' Various reviewers singled out the title story for praise. The *Times* critic, who pointed out that short stories usually 'depend for much of their effect on the actual texture of the writing', found that the opening sentence, 'with its almost breathless flow of information, its unmistakably working-class tone, its invocation of the law as something undesirable ... is a perfect earnest for the story which follows.' And Eric Moon in the *Saturday Review* was moved by Sillitoe's 'curiously convincing blending of his usual realism and passion with a lyrical romanticism' in the story, a quality he felt could be seen clearly in the 'scene where Doris ... rides through a depressing slum area to meet [her working-class lover] ... on a snow-white horse.'

Comments in other reviews suggested a continuing unease about authorial intrusion in Sillitoe's fiction. In the view of Mordecai Richler, 'the author's rage seems to influence and manipulate too many of his characters [and] at times he appears to lecture at us through everybody.' A partial explanation for this phenomenon may be found in Sillitoe's closeness to his material. Not only is he concerned in the early fiction with teaching his readers a lesson in social morality, but as Karl Miller suggested, he is creating in his books 'a running celebration of his own kin or dynasty. He is the archivist of the sly, battling Sillitoes and in his foremost works he has done them proud.' Yet as Miller perceptively concluded, Sillitoe could not 'take his ancestor-worship much further. The propitiations have been achieved, the archives completed.' Most of those who reviewed *The Ragman's Daughter* felt the same way.

A careful reading of the reviews of Sillitoe's early fiction suggests two important conclusions. First, it is clear that in his early novels and stories Sillitoe succeeded in fostering a public awareness and discussion of the social issues which were of vital importance to him; second, that the assessments of his earliest critical readers, taken collectively, not only help to define his social vision for us, but also, by discussing aspects of his technical competence, aid in our evaluation of the quality of his art. As Richard Altick reminded us in his revised edition of *The Art of Literary Research*, it is important to view a writer's work from every conceivable angle of vision in order to arrive at a balanced assessment of his achievement. The fresh critical perceptions of reviewers, so often overlooked, can and do provide information about a writer's work not to be found elsewhere. In the case of Alan Sillitoe, they have proved particularly illuminating, serving to confirm and amplify the working-class perspectives that inform some of his best work.

Notes and References

[1] Reviews quoted in this chapter are listed in the bibliography.

Chapter Eight

Masters and Men:
The Literary Tradition of the Working-class Hero

Few reviewers of the Nottingham fiction gave any indication that Sillitoe was working in a well-defined though minor literary tradition in the creation and presentation of his working-class heroes. Yet such a tradition does exist, and an awareness of its fundamental character is important to a full appreciation of Sillitoe's early novels and stories. The present chapter documents the tradition and assesses some of the more significant incarnations of the working-class hero in English fiction preceding the publication of *Saturday Night and Sunday Morning* in 1958.

For practical purposes, we can trace the beginnings of the working-class hero in the English novel to the mid-1840's. The Industrial Revolution had contributed to the increasingly urbanised character of English society, and the growth of the great industrial towns was well under way, with large urban slums already much in evidence. Living conditions for the working-class families who inhabited these areas were often appalling, and growing discontent among the workers, based on a strong feeling that they were being exploited by factory owners, pointed to confrontations between representatives of Labour and Capital. With the raw material of a potentially explosive social situation at hand, it was inevitable that novelists would begin to recognise its dramatic literary possibilities. Throughout the 1840's and 1850's a number of writers attempted to meet the challenge of this new material. The most prominent among them were the Earl of Beaconsfield, Benjamin Disraeli, who published *Sybil* in 1845 and with his subtitle, *The Two Nations*, suggested a useful focus which the novel develops; Elizabeth Gaskell, who attempted to define the working-class point of view in *Mary Barton* (1848) and *North and South* (1855); and Charles Dickens, who produced in *Hard Times* (1854) the most famous condemnation of industrialism to come out of the period.[1]

In an advertisement prefacing *Sybil* Disraeli alluded to 'the subject which these volumes aim to illustrate – the Condition of the People.' According to P. J. Keating in *The working classes in Victorian fiction*, *Sybil* and the novels of Mrs Gaskell and Dickens are propagandist, 'written by authors who are not working-class, for an audience which is not working-class, and [in which] character and environment are presented so as to contain, implicitly or explicitly, a class judgement. The author may wish to show, for instance, that the working-classes are ... not at heart violent and so long as their just complaints are listened to sympathetically the middle and upper classes have nothing to fear from them. Or even more directly, that they need help, that they shouldn't drink, that more schools, hospitals or workhouses ... should be built for them.' In each of the novels mentioned, the writers rely heavily on the actions and particularly on the statements of their characters to make their social theses clear. That is to say, fictional working-class men and women in the industrial novels of the forties and fifties are first and foremost representatives of their class. Although they may be allowed to exhibit individual differences of temperament or attitude, they function primarily as spokesmen for class grievances and class loyalties. As Keating has suggested, 'the most important single fact about the [Victorian] fictional working man is his class.' The more prominent among them, those characters articulate and active enough to enjoy the role of heroes, inevitably stand out by their strong sense of class solidarity and by their aggrieved and often hostile reaction to treatment of the working man that they regard as either inequitable or unjust.

The basic dichotomy between the working-class and others is made clear in *Sybil* by Stephen Morley, 'a workman, and the son of a workman', who also writes for a radical Midlands paper, the *Mowbray Phalanx*. He tells Charles Egremont, the well-to-do second son of an aristocratic family, that the Queen rules over 'two nations, between whom there is no intercourse and no sympathy; who are as ignorant of each other's habits, thoughts, and feelings, as if they were dwellers in different zones, or inhabitants of different planets; who are formed by a different breeding, are fed by a different food, are ordered by different manners, and are not governed by the same laws.' He concludes, not very originally, by labelling these groups the Rich and the Poor. More particular description of the condition of the industrial poor, or working-class, is given by Walter Gerard, Sybil's father. Gerard, who is variously described as 'a workman at a factory' and an 'overlooker at Mr Trafford's mill', is an atheist and a man of outspoken views. As he sees it, the position of his fellow factory workers is little better than that of slaves. He tells Egremont: 'there is more serfdom in England now than at any time since the Conquest. I speak of what passes under my daily eyes when I say, that those who labour can as little choose or change their masters now, as when they were born thralls. There are great bodies of the working classes of this country nearer the condition of brutes than they have been at any time since the Conquest.' He goes on to speak of the prevalence of disease among the working poor, encouraged by overcrowded and unsanitary living conditions: 'We have more pestilence now in England than we ever had, but it only reaches the poor. You never hear of it. Why, Typhus alone takes every year from the dwellings of the artisan and peasant a population equal to that of the whole county of Westmoreland.' Elsewhere he speaks movingly of 'the married life of a woman of our class, [which] in the present condition of our country, is a lease of woe ... [they are] slaves, and the slaves of slaves.'

Walter Gerard is not only an articulate spokesman on the subject of working-class grievances and rights, he is also a political activist whose revolutionary fervour results in his being imprisoned for sedition. For him the political and social status quo, in which workers were denied justice in the form of fairer pay and access to better working and living conditions, is intolerable. Setting a precedent for later working-class heroes, he hints at future class confrontation if the workers are not listened to. They are justified, he argues, in demanding 'their rights, rights consistent with the rights of other classes, but without which the rights of other classes cannot and ought not to be secure.' Gerard is also capable of prescient analysis of the workers' condition. He speaks to Egremont, for example, of 'wages weekly dropping, and just work enough to hinder sheer idleness; that sort of thing keeps the people in very humble trim. But wait a bit, and when they have reached starvation point, I fancy we shall hear a murmur.' The fancied murmur in this case turns out to be a violent strike. Gerard, who is not at first directly involved, argues skilfully with the strikers against the destruction of Trafford's mill on the grounds that public sympathy for their cause will not be won by wanton vandalism. He is listened to, and the protesting workers than move towards the grounds of a nearby stately home for a peaceful demonstration. There they are confronted with a detachment of militia, who have been called in to assist the local mill owners. Suddenly, without cause, 'the people were fired on and sabred. The indignant spirit of Gerard resisted; he struck down a trooper to the earth, and incited those about him not to yield. The father of Sybil was [then] picked out, the real friend and champion of the People, and shot dead.'

The violent death of Walter Gerard dramatically underscores Disraeli's thesis about the existence of 'two nations' in English society. At the same time it suggests a certain pessimism about the perpetuation of that division, at least until 'the condition of the People' is more completely understood. Nonetheless, *Sybil* may be considered the first significant attempt in English fiction to bridge the gulf of ignorance between Rich and Poor, and Walter Gerard remains the pioneer fictional spokesman for the working-class.

In *Mary Barton* (1848), the first novel of Elizabeth Gaskell, we are offered a more fully developed working-class hero in the figure of John Barton, the central character. Professor A. W. Ward, introducing the 1906 reprint of the novel, quotes from a letter written by Mrs Gaskell to Mrs W. R. Greg, in which the significance of Barton is made clear: 'Round the character of John Barton all the others formed themselves; he was my hero, *the* person with whom all my sympathies went ... because I believed from personal observation that such men were not uncommon, and would well reward such sympathy and love as should throw light down upon their groping search after the causes of suffering.' In an attempt to illuminate the general causes of working-class suffering in the novel, Mrs Gaskell gives the reader a long series of particular descriptions of the hardships of Barton's own life. To begin with, his credentials as a legitimate representative of the working-class are carefully established. We are told that he was 'born of factory workers, and himself bred up in youth, and living in manhood, among the mills' as a weaver. He is described as being 'below the middle size and slightly made; there was almost a stunted look about him; and his wan, colourless face, gave you the idea, that in his childhood he had suffered from the scanty living consequent upon bad times, and improvident habits.' Then the seriousness of his character is asserted as we are told that his 'features were strongly marked, though not irregular, and their expression was extreme earnestness, resolute either for good or evil, a sort of latent stern enthusiasm.' We may read this partly as an attempt to convince the reader that Barton's opinions are considered and worth our attention, but also as a reinforcement of the idea that for the suffering poor, life is a grim business indeed. At this point we are ready to react to Barton's troubles and to see them, by extension, as representative troubles of the working-class.

For much of the novel's time span John Barton is out of work or on short time, the mills being often idle because of low demand for cotton goods and an unwillingness on the part of the owners to sell at drastically reduced prices. Barton's assessment of the situation and the suffering it caused is evident as he tells his friend George Wilson, 'You'll say ... they'n getten capital an' we'n getten none. I say, our labour's our capital, and we ought to draw interest on that. They get interest on their capital somehow a' this time, while ourn is lying idle, else how could they all live as they do? ... They'n screwed us down to th' lowest peg, in order to make their great big fortunes, and build their great big houses, and we, why we're just clemming [starving], many and many of us. Can you say there's nought wrong in this?' Partly because of his way with words, John Barton is chosen by his fellow workers as a delegate to petition Parliament for relief on account of widespread hardship caused by the extended shutdown of the mills. Parliament refuses to meet the delegation, however, and its members are also harassed by the London police. They return home bitter and despairing.

Echoing Walter Gerard's sense of alienation from those in positions of power and authority, Barton feels that 'we're their slaves as long as we can work; we pile up their fortunes with the sweat of our brows, and yet we are to live as separate as if we were in two worlds ... with a great gulf betwixt us.' The extent of this division between *them* and *us* is made graphically clear during a prolonged period of un-employment when Barton's son falls desperately ill of scarlet fever. Hungry and desperate for food and fuel to comfort his boy, he wanders into the town and sees his ex-employer's wife come out of an expensive shop 'loaded with purchases for a party.' Barton 'returned home with a bitter spirit of wrath in his heart, to see his only boy a corpse.' Though the scene may be contrived and melodramatic, it does offer a compelling personal reason for Barton's vehement attacks on 'gentlefolk': 'And what good have they ever done me that I should like them? [he cries out].... If I am sick do they come and nurse me? If my child lies dying ... does the rich man bring the wine or broth that might save his life? If I am out of work for weeks in the bad times, and winter comes, with black frost, and keen east wind, and there is no coal for the grate, and no clothes for the bed, and the thin bones are seen through the ragged clothes, does the rich man share his plenty with me, as he ought to do, if his religion wasn't a humbug? . . . Don't think to come over me with th' old tale, that the rich know nothing of the trials of the poor; I say, if they don't know, they ought to know.'

The attempt to make them know leads to the novel's climax. At a rare meeting between mill owners and men, Harry Carson, the son of an owner, draws caricatures of the workers on a scrap of paper which he idly tosses aside. It is picked up by one of the men, and shown to John Barton. At a subsequent meeting Barton uses the incident to incite his fellow workers to violence: 'It makes me more than sad, it makes my heart burn within me, to see that folk can make a jest of striving men; of chaps who comed to ask for a bit o' fire for th' old granny, as shivers i' th' cold; for a bit o' bedding, and some warm clothing to the poor wife who lies in labour on th' damp flags; and for victuals for the childer, whose little voices are getting too faint and weak to cry aloud wi' hunger. For brothers, is not them the things we ask for when we ask for more wage?' He finishes his speech with a powerful peroration, guaranteed to move the men to action: 'We donnot want dainties, we want bellyfuls; we donnot want gimcrack coats and waist-coats, we want warm clothes. . . . We donnot want their grand houses, we want a roof to cover us from the rain, and the snow, and the storm, ay, and not alone to cover us, but the helpless ones that cling to us in the keen wind, and ask us with their eyes why we brought 'em into th' world to suffer?' As he finishes, Barton twice exhorts the men to 'Have at the masters!' The dramatic result is a secret plan to kill Harry Carson, followed by a drawing of lots to determine the murderer. Barton himself draws the marked lot. Although he is able to commit the murder, it is his final gesture of defiance against the class that victimised him for so long. Soon after, overcome by the effects of prolonged taking of opium to ease his suffering, and stricken by conscience at the enormity of his act, he lapses into illness and dies a broken man,

Mrs Gaskell's second working-class spokesman, Nicholas Higgins in *North and South* (1855), plays a less prominent role than John Barton in the earlier novel. Nonetheless, he shares Barton's strong sense of class solidarity, and is pointed and articulate in his denunciation of what he sees as unjust treatment of working men and their families. His views are expressed for the most part in conversation with Margaret Hale, the novel's independent middle-class heroine who has recently moved with her parents to the 'Darkshire' industrial town of Milton Northern. When they first meet, Higgins exhibits a talent ascribed to a number of later working-class heroes, including Sillitoe's, the ability to assess a new acquaintance quickly. 'I can read her proud bonny face like a book', he tells his daughter Bessy, and Margaret is immediately impressed with 'the man's insight into what had been passing in her mind.' She continues to be impressed in later conversations, particularly with Higgins' cogent articulation of the working man's point of view regarding his relationship with his employers. Underlying his position is the workers' pride: 'Almost the best words that men can say', he tells her, are ' "Gi' me work", [which] means "and I'll do it like a man".' Then there is the workers' interpretation of class roles played by employer and employee, or 'masters and men': 'I'll tell yo' it's their part ... to beat us down, to swell their fortunes; and it's ours to stand up and fight hard – not for ourselves alone, but for them round about us – for justice and fair play. We help to make their profits, and we ought to help spend 'em.' Elsewhere Higgins calls the mill owners tyrants and argues that only through Unions can the workers hope to oppose their tyranny successfully. 'It's a withstanding of injustice, past, present, or to come.... Our only chance is binding men together in one common interest ... [in a Union] whose only strength is in numbers.'

Higgins is active in Union affairs and displays a bellicosity that characterises many working-class heroes as he helps prepare for a strike which has been called because the principal mill owners want to lower wages. 'We know when we're put upon', he tells Margaret, 'and we'en too much blood in us to stand it. We just take our hand fro' our looms, and say, "Yo' may clem us, but yo'll not put upon us, my masters!" And be danged to 'em, they shan't this time!' His tenacious belief in the justice of the workers' cause leads him to speak of looking 'forward to the chance of dying at my post sooner than yield.' He compares his position to that of a soldier, 'only, m'appen, the cause he dies for it's just that of somebody he never clapt eyes on, nor heerd on all his born days, while I take up John Boucher's cause, as lives next door but one, wi' a sickly wife, and eight childer, none on 'em factory age; and I don't take up his cause only ... but I take up th' cause of justice.' Though he loses his job as a result of his activities as a Union leader, Nicholas Higgins ultimately fares better than either Walter Gerard or John Barton. At the close of the novel he has found work with a more understanding mill owner, one who is convinced by Margaret Hale that the leaders of the strike were 'steady thoughtful men; good hands, and good citizens, who were friendly to law and judgement, and would uphold order; who only wanted their right wage, and wouldn't work [for less], even though they starved.'

It is clear that in *North and South* Mrs Gaskell embraced the utopian view that workers and factory owners could solve a great many of their mutual problems by coming to know one another personally. Her contemporary, Charles Dickens, offered a less sanguine view in *Hard Times* (1854). Set in Coketown, 'that ugly citadel' of industry, *Hard Times* records the personal troubles of Stephen Blackpool, a middle-aged power loom weaver. He is described as 'a man of perfect integrity' and 'quiet, watchful and steady.' At forty, he 'looked older, but he had had a hard life. ... A rather stooping man, with a knitted brow, a pondering expression of face, and a hard-looking head sufficiently capacious, on which his iron-grey hair lay long and thin.' Unlike the working-class representatives in other industrial novels, Stephen Blackpool is a passive victim, acted on by the economic forces that control his life, but unwilling to rebel against them to alter his situation. Legally bound in marriage to a woman who went to the bad and left him years before, and unable to marry Rachel, the woman he loves, Stephen finally resolves after years of patient suffering to approach the mill owner, Josiah Bounderby, for advice.

Unfortunately, Bounderby has a biased view of the 'hands' who work in his factory, suspecting them all, 'man, woman, or child', to have 'one ultimate object in life. That object is, to be fed on turtle soup and venison with a gold spoon.' His advice, that the only way to divorce is through complex legal proceedings costing perhaps £1,500, dramatically points up for Stephen and the reader the privileges of the well-off and the plight of the working poor. The idea is reinforced as Stephen speaks of the 'black unpassable world' between those in positions of power and the workers when he is being questioned later by Bounderby on Union organisation in the factory. In the presence of the local member of Parliament, Stephen attempts to explain the workers' predicament: 'Deed we are in a muddle, Sir. Look round town – so rich as 'tis – and see the numbers o' people as has been broughten into bein' heer, fur to weave, an' to card, an' to piece out a livin', aw the same one way, somehows 'twixt their cradles and their graves. Look how we live, an' wheer we live, an' in what numbers, an' by what chances, and wi' what sameness; and look how the mills is awlus a goin, and how they never works us no nigher to onny dis'ant object – ceptin awlus, Death. Look how you considers of us ... how you are awlus right, and how we are awlus wrong, and never had'n no reason in us sin ever we were born.' More particularly Stephen expresses his worry about dehumanising views of the workers held by men such as those he is addressing: 'most o' aw, rating 'em as so much Power, and reg'latin 'em as if they was figures in a soom, or machines; wi'out lives and likens, wi'out memories and inclinations, wi'out souls to weary and souls to hope.' The result of Stephen's unguarded response is predictable: he is summarily dismissed as a dangerous advocate of workers' rights. Later, returning home at night from looking for work in a nearby town, he falls into an unmarked, abandoned mine shaft and is killed.

It is ironic that Stephen's one attempt to set the record straight, to explain in his hesitant resigned manner the social problems he sees around him, leads to his victimisation and indirectly to his death. Though Stephen Blackpool may have been unable to alter the social and economic position of the workers, he nevertheless fulfils an important function: like the working-class spokesmen of other industrial novels, he has made countless readers aware of the existence of injustice and inequality, affirming once again that 'attention must be paid.'

While the perspective of the factory worker is encountered most often in fiction about the English working-class, it is not the only one explored by Victorian novelists. A number of writers, including Charles Kingsley, George Eliot and Mark Rutherford, deal with the views of 'intellectual' working men, generally tradesmen such as tailors or printers who come from working-class homes and work in small shops. Such men are normally represented as being intellectually superior to their fellows and strongly committed to improving the conditions of working-class life. In Kingsley's *Alton Locke* (1850), Eliot's *Felix Holt* (1886) and Rutherford's *The Revolution in Tanner's Lane* (1887) the typical pattern is for the hero to immerse himself in a regimen of reading and study that leads to his becoming much better educated than his work-mates, and then to involve himself passionately in various kinds of political activity on their behalf. Alton Locke, for example, becomes involved in writing for radical papers and in organising political demonstrations, while Zachariah Coleman (*The Revolution in Tanner's Lane*) is active in an underground revolutionary group called The Friends of the People. And in each of the novels mentioned, the hero is sent to prison for taking part in violent demonstrations on behalf of workers' rights. Unhappily these intellectual working-class heroes rarely come to life, despite their involvement in dramatic situations. The heroes of the industrial novels, while obviously manipulated to support certain theories of class interaction, were nonetheless credible characters and convincing representatives of their class. The intellectual workers of Kingsley, Eliot and Rutherford, on the other hand, are cardboard figures who fail to engage our sympathies. Barbara Hardy, in her critical study entitled *The Novels of George Eliot*, calls Felix Holt 'a lifeless character, except in local flashes', and the judgement may be applied equally to Alton Locke and Zachariah Coleman. The reason is not hard to find. As these heroes become increasingly engaged in political activity, they lose touch with the milieu which produced them and originally motivated their political involvement. As they spend more and more time travelling and arguing the workers' cause with middle-class and aristocratic adversaries, they become theory-spouting puppets, detached from the immediate realities of working-class life.

The process may be seen in each of the three novels considered here. At the close of each novel the hero has moved a long way from his original position advocating mass protest by the workers. As Zachariah Coleman unsuccessfully seeks work early in *The Revolution in Tanner's Lane*, Rutherford tells the reader: 'Those of us who have craved unsuccessfully for permission to do what the Maker of us all fitted us to do alone understand how revolutions are generated. ... Let no man judge communist or anarchist *till he has asked for leave to work*, and a "Damn your eyes!" has rung in his ears.' Coleman himself, asserting 'I believe in insurrection', argues that 'insurrection strengthens the belief of men in the right. ... When a company of poor men meet together and declare that things have got to such a pass they will either kill their enemies or die themselves, the world then thinks there must, after all, be *some* difference between right and wrong.' But Zachariah Coleman eventually becomes disillusioned, and quits all political activity to devote his life fully to his new young wife and daughter. Felix Holt, who supports a miners' strike and dreams of becoming a national spokesman for them, demands a substantial change in the political power structure. 'I want the working men to have power. I'm a working man myself, and I don't want to be anything else. ... I hope we, or the children that come after us, will get plenty of political power.' But after serving a prison term for his part in a violent demonstration, his position is dramatically altered: 'If there's anything our people want convincing of', he says, 'it is, that there's some dignity and happiness for a man other than changing his station.' And at the end of the novel 'the demagogue has become a local, small-time teacher.' Alton Locke, who begins as a 'Cockney among Cockneys' and 'a poet of the people', eventually accepts the invitation of Lady Ellerton, a former opponent, to travel to the South Pacific in search of evidence to justify a theory of human brotherhood. In the end all three intellectual working-class heroes are in varying degrees untrue to their class. For the reader they have become hollow men who no longer function either as credible characters or as convincing interpreters of working-class attitudes.

In the history of working-class literature the fiction of George Gissing occupies an important place. Five of his first seven novels are about working-class life: *Workers in the Dawn* (1880), *The Unclassed* (1884), *Demos* (1886), *Thyrza* (1887) and *The Nether World* (1889). But as P. J. Keating points out, in only two of these, *Demos* and *The Nether World*, are the protagonists genuine working men. In the others they are displaced intellectuals from other classes who are or who become financially independent and have little in common with those with whom they associate in the slums. Arthur Golding (*Workers in the Dawn*) is born in working-class surroundings because of his father's social and economic descent through alcoholism, but as Keating notes, 'by virtue of his exceptional sensitivity he stands outside a working-class way of life.' He becomes an artist, and on the receipt of an inheritance is able to leave the slums and follow his career elsewhere. Osmond Waymark (*The Unclassed*) has an independent income and spends time in a working-class milieu, as a school-teacher and rent collector, to study its inhabitants in order to write novels about them. And Walter Egremont (*Thyrza*) makes his contact with the working-class by giving them evening lectures on English literature to improve their minds. On the other hand Richard Mutimer (*Demos*) and Sidney Kirkwood (*The Nether World*) are authentic working men, though both are better situated than many of their class. Mutimer is a 'mechanical engineer', who repairs malfunctioning factory equipment, and Kirkwood spends his working hours assembling and repairing jewellery in the workroom of a shop. Of the two, Mutimer is clearly the more compelling and forceful.

It is well known that Gissing harboured ambivalent attitudes towards the working-class inhabitants of slum districts in London were he was forced to live for a number of years. This is particularly evident in the fiction in *Demos*, in his portrait of Richard Mutimer. Although Gissing tells us that Mutimer represents 'the best qualities his class can show', the compliment carries more than a hint of condescension. The reader is soon made to see that although Mutimer is superior to his fellows in some ways, he is also, like them, the victim of a peculiarly limited upbringing. His uncritical, aggressive outlook on life, for example, was bred into him from an early age, for 'the chosen directors of his prejudice taught him to regard every fact, every discovery, as for or against something.' And although like other working-class heroes he is very observant, Gissing reminds us that his eyes 'seemed to be always looking for the weak points of whatever they regarded, and their brightness was not seldom suggestive of malice.'

This combination of belligerence and critical myopia marks Richard Mutimer throughout the novel. When we meet him at the age of twenty-five he has just lost his job for 'making all his mates discontented and calling his employers names at every street corner'.[2] Zealous in the Socialist cause, and frequently called on to speak at meetings because of his 'uncompromising rhetoric', 'he believed himself about to become a popular hero; already in imagination he stood forth on platforms before vast assemblies, and heard his own voice denouncing capitalism with force which nothing could resist.' The chance to make his mark in the battle against capitalism comes sooner than he expects. As the nearest relative of a self-made industrialist who has supposedly died intestate, Mutimer suddenly finds himself wealthy. In a scheme calculated to 'shame those dunderheaded, callous-hearted aristocrats [and] those ravening bourgeois', he embarks upon an ambitious socialist experiment. His plan is to establish a utopian industrial community at New Wanley in the Midlands, with smelters and engineering works and houses for the men, in an enterprise designed to run for the benefit of the workers and with profits to be used to finance socialist propaganda.

At the beginning of the undertaking Mutimer sees himself as 'the glorified respresentative of his class', promising a London socialist meeting to 'use every opportunity that's given me to uphold the cause of the poor and down-trodden against the rich and selfish and luxurious, [so] that if I live another fifty years I shall still be of the people and with the people.' His passionate conviction that the working-class is treated unjustly in capitalist society is made clear shortly after his arrival at New Wanley, when he proclaims to a middle-class audience:

> the man who lives on wages is never free; he sells himself body and soul to his employer. What sort of freedom does a man enjoy who may any day find himself and his family on the point of starvation just because he has lost his work? All his life long he has before his mind the fear of want – not only of straitened means, mind you, but of destitution and the workhouse. How can such a man put aside his common cares? Religion is a luxury; the working man has no luxuries. Now speak of the free evenings.... Do you understand what that free evening means? He gets home, say, at six o'clock, tired out; he has to be up again perhaps at five next morning. What can he do but just lie about half asleep? Why, that's the whole principle of the capitalist system of employment; it's calculated exactly how long a man can be made to work in a day without making him in-

capable of beginning again on the day following – just as it's calculated exactly how little a man can live upon, in the regulation of wages. . . . The principle is that a man shall have no strength left for himself; it's all paid for, every scrap of it, bought with the wages at week end.

After he has been at New Wanley for a time, however, Richard Mutimer's sympathies begin to shift. In a series of sharply etched vignettes Gissing shows him ashamed of his unsophisticated family, turning away from his former friends, rejecting his working-class fiancée in favour of a more socially acceptable woman from the middle class, and firing one of his workers for impudence. The extent of his alienation from his origins becomes clear with the unexpected appearance of his uncle's will, which effectively disinherits him. Forced to return to his former working-class milieu, Mutimer flings himself once again into socialist politics. In a dramatic moment of self-analysis, however, he recognises that he can no longer claim to represent his class: 'now he belonged to no class at all; he was a professional agitator, and must remain so through his life – or till the Revolution came.' Dreaming of becoming the 'First President of the English Republic', he becomes instead a demagogue of the London slums. In the end he rejects the working-class completely. Chased by an angry mob because of his involvement in a fraudulent savings scheme in which large numbers of workers had lost money, he cries out: 'Listen to them! That's the People, that is! I deserve killing, fool that I am, if only for the lying good I've said of them.' Moments later he is killed, struck in the temple by a heavy stone thrown by one of the workers.

In *Demos* Gissing's treatment of the working-class hero was essentially satiric, attempting to show that the working man, however committed to his class he might seem to be, was likely to betray it given half a chance. It was also extremely pessimistic, suggesting there was little likelihood of any amelioration of the workers' lot in the foreseeable future. Further evidence of this pessimistic outlook may be found in *The Nether World*, Gissing's second novel to use a genuine working man as its hero. Sidney Kirkwood is a different kind of hero, however, both less dynamic and less vocal than his counterpart in the earlier work. His role is primarily that of the quiet Good Samaritan, helping those of his acquaintances who are too poor, old, suffering or desperate to help themselves. At first, given the graphic portrayals of the Clerkenwell (London) milieu and the representations of minor characters which are among the most memorable in working-class fiction, the characterisation of Kirkwood seems particularly weak. There is little evidence of the restless drive that characterised Richard Mutimer, and no suggestion that he is to play a dominant role in the novel. In fact, contemporary reviewers largely ignored his existence, though in an introduction to the 1880 'Colonial Edition' of the novel a critic who signed himself P. R. called him 'in some sort the workaday hero of the more sentimental part of the story.' Nonetheless, Sidney Kirkwood had a meaningful role to play in Gissing's interpretation of working-class life, and this is evident in the final passage of the novel, in which he speaks of Kirkwood and Jane Snowden, the heroine: 'In each life [there was] little for congratulation. . . . Yet to both was their work given. Unmarked, unencouraged save by their love of uprightness and mercy, they stood by the side of those more hapless, brought some comfort to hearts less courageous than their own. Where they abode it was not all dark. Sorrow certainly awaited them, perchance defeat in even the humble aims that they had set themselves; but at least their lives would remain a protest against those brute forces of society which fill with wreck the abysses of the nether world.'

It is evident that Gissing's pessimism about the ability of working-class men and women to improve their situation in any significant and permanent manner remains unaltered in his final novel of working-class life. In *Demos* Richard Mutimer, illustrating 'the best qualities his class can show', is nonetheless alienated from that class and destroyed. Sidney Kirkwood allows his initiative to be suppressed and becomes a nursemaid to the suffering poor, ministering to the effects of 'those brute forces of society' which contribute to working-class misery, but remaining content to ignore the causes. Although the sardonic pessimism of *Demos* is tempered in *The Nether World* by a mood of quiet resignation, the working-class hero is used primarily in both novels to dramatise Gissing's scorn for working-class attitudes and aspirations.

In the decade following publication of *The Nether World* the English working-class became for a time a literary fashion, providing subject matter for numerous novels and short stories. Though many of these works were merely sentimental romances set in working-class surroundings, or thinly disguised moral tracts, there were also a number of serious attempts to record with accuracy the activities and attitudes of working-class men and women. Of these, the best known and most influential were written by Arthur Morrison, whose *Tales of Mean Streets* (1894) triggered an extended debate on the realistic representation of violence in working-class fiction. His later work included two novels about contemporary working-class life in London's East End, *A Child of the Jago* (1896) and *To London Town* (1899) as well as an historical novel entitled *A Hole in the Wall* (1902) which utilised the same background. Together with *Tales of Mean Streets* they offered a detailed, composite picture of late Victorian working-class life in a rigidly demarcated setting.

Morrison, who lived for long periods in the slums he describes with careful accuracy, comes closer in these novels to conveying a sustained sense of felt life than any of the writers discussed earlier in this chapter. In Morrison's work the reader is convinced that he is being given an insider's picture of working-class life, with its dreary monotony, highly developed code of what is respectable and what is not, and frequent explosions of violence. This impression is supported by Morrison's ability to let the events speak for themselves so that the reader is left to interpret their significance in his own way. In other words, the representation of working-class life is not obviously coloured by the author's social or moral theses about that life, nor is it filtered through the prejudiced sensibility of a hero who is merely a mouthpiece for the author. In each of Morrison's three working-class novels, according to P. J. Keating, 'the central character is a child who is faced with the problem of how to escape from the lower strata of working-class life,' and in each case he fails. Dicky Perrott in *A Child of the Jago*, for example, is killed by his arch-enemy, a neighbourhood hunchback, and Johnny May in *To London Town* is caught by his love for Nora, the daughter of old Mother Born-drunk, a degraded drunken slut. In each case the child or young man is faced with a series of immediate problems with which he copes in some fashion, but he is unable to see them in a larger perspective, to perceive his long-term dilemma. In Morrison's work the hero as he was present in earlier working-class fiction, as spokesman for working-class rights or chronicler of injustice, simply does not exist. As Keating says of Morrison's first novel, 'in *A Child of the Jago*, the Jago [setting] itself is the true hero.'

A similar judgement might be applied to Morrison's later novels, as well as to Somerset Maugham's novel of working-class life, *Liza of Lambeth* (1897). In fact R. L. Calder hints at this in his critical study entitled *W. Somerset Maugham and the Quest for Freedom* when he says: 'like ... Morrison's "Jago", Vere Street [the principal setting in *Liza of Lambeth*] is treated almost as a character, and it is a powerful force.' Calder goes on to stress the strong influence of Morrison on Maugham, analysing the predicament of Maugham's central character, a girl overwhelmed by the rigid demands of society in a confined working-class milieu, and concludes that 'just as the "Jago" has Dicky Perrott [in its grip], Vere Street has Liza Kemp.'

The conventional working-class hero, having been temporarily eclipsed by the powerfully drawn local settings in the fiction of Morrison and Maugham, makes a memorable reappearance in the work of Robert Tressell. In *The Ragged Trousered Philanthropists* (1914) the setting is of secondary importance. Instead, the reader's attention is directed to the workers themselves, and particularly to Frank Owen, a tubercular house painter who is the novel's hero. Owen's origins are solidly working-class: he is the son of a journeyman carpenter and a mother who earns 'a scanty living as a needle-woman' after her husband's early death. At the age of thirteen Owen is apprenticed to a master decorator, and spends the rest of his life employed by Rushton and Co., a contracting and renovations firm. Since Rushton's clients are invariably well-to-do, there is plenty of opportunity for Owen and his fellow workers to compare the world of wealth they see on the job and the world of poverty they live in at home. The former is inhabited by men with evocative, Dickensian names such as Starvem, Didlum, Sweater and Grinder. In the middle are their working-class minions who act as foremen on the various jobs. Among them are the hypocritical Mr Hunter, nicknamed 'Misery' for his brutal treatment of the men, and Crass, who 'did as little work as possible himself, [though] he took care that the others worked hard.' The latter world is made up of the workers, who are paid between four and a half pence and eight pence an hour, and who live in constant fear of losing their jobs: 'Everyone was afraid. They knew that this man Misery had the power to deprive them of the means of earning a living – that he possessed the power to deprive their children of bread.'

Frank Owen, who shares the indignities and anxieties of his fellows but unlike many of them appreciates the social significance of their suffering, is clearly intended by Tressell to be a spokesman for social reform. As an atheist he is convinced that there is no unalterable divine plan for society, and argues passionately for a revision of the social status quo. On a personal level he agonises over the death of a fellow worker who is killed after being forced to work on unsafe scaffolding, and over the starvation of an older worker who was fired without cause so that another man could be hired more cheaply, and he worries constantly about the future of his wife and son should he lose his own work. At times he is 'disheartened', feeling 'like a beaten dog', and 'oppressed by a sense of impotence and shameful degradation.' There are moments too when he is angered to the edge of violence. Reacting on one occasion to Misery's tyranny, 'he felt that he would like to take him by the throat with one hand and smash his face in with the other.' Most depressing of all for Owen personally is the recognition that 'all his life it had been the same: incessant work under similar more or less humiliating conditions, and with no more result than being just able to avoid starvation. And the future, as far as he could see, was as hopeless as the past.'

On a more abstract level, Owen's assessment of the social dilemma comprehends both conventional and original ideas. On the one hand, he rails against employers who 'rob the workers of the greater part of the fruits of their toil', and argues that as the workers do their 'full share of the work, therefore we should have a full share of things that are made by work.' He also castigates 'Employers – or rather Exploiters – of Labour, Thieves, Swindlers, Pickpockets, profit-seeking Shareholders, Burglars, Bishops, Financiers [and] Capitalists' as enemies of the working-class. At the firm's annual outing, a country pub crawl by chartered bus, he listens to Mr Rushton speak of a natural 'division of labour; the men worked with their hands and the masters worked with their brains, and one was no use without the other.' In an impassioned response he refutes Rushton's assertion, pointing out that after twenty years in business an employer is set up for life, while his workmen have nothing. In the political arena Owen campaigns actively for the Socialists, giving lectures and handing out pamphlets on the street and at meetings held by the Liberal and Conservative parties. On the other hand – and here Owen is set apart from other working-class heroes – he recognises that the workers themselves must share the responsibility for their situation. Although he feels that 'the majority work hard and live in poverty in order that the minority may live in luxury without working at all', he concludes that this is true partly because 'the majority are mostly fools.' In Owen's view the workers are philanthropists, donating their time and labour in the service of others, though ironically their efforts are directed to helping those who need it least. The workers' passivity in accepting their lot, and their unwillingness to form a union to improve con-

ditions of employment, are acutely frustrating to the perceptive, reformist Owen:

> *They were the enemy* – those ragged trousered philan-
> thropists who not only quietly submitted like so many
> cattle to their miserable slavery for the benefit of others,
> but defended it, and opposed and ridiculed any sugges-
> tion of reform. *They were the real oppressors* – the men
> who spoke of themselves as 'the likes of us', who, having
> lived in poverty and degradation all their lives, con-
> sidered that what had been good enough for them was
> good enough for the children they had been the means
> of bringing into existence.... It was their apathy or
> active opposition that made it impossible to establish a
> better system of society, under which those who did
> their fair share of the world's work would be honoured
> and rewarded.

Partly because of the workers' apathy, Owen develops a
revolutionary fervour that demands a complete transforma-
tion of society: 'there's so much the matter with the present
system that it's no good tinkering at it. Everything about it
is wrong and there's nothing about it that's right. There's
only one thing to be done with it and that is to smash it up
and have a different system altogether.' At the end of the
novel Owen dreams of a Co-operative Commonwealth, a
'State in which no ... man will find his profit in another's
loss, and we shall no longer be masters and servants ... where
there will be no weary, broken men and women passing their
joyless lives in toil and want, and no little children crying
because they are hungry and cold.' It seems unlikely, however, that Owen will live to see his dream come true. The
rapid and inexorable progression of his tuberculosis makes
his death seem imminent as the novel draws to a close.

To place Frank Owen in the tradition of the working-class
hero, one must remember that like earlier heroes he is defined
by his class – it is the single most important fact about him.
And like Gissing's heroes in *Demos* and *The Nether World*,

he is an authentic representative of his class. But Owen is more than this. Partly because Robert Tressell had lived the life he recreates for his hero – there is a remarkable series of parallels between the experiences of author and character – partly because of Owen's own prejudiced view of his fellow workers as co-authors of their own predicament, Frank Owen stands out as the most compelling and convincing interpreter of the working-class condition to appear in English fiction before the First World War.

In the period between the wars the work of three novelists merits some attention: they are Henry Green, Walter Greenwood and James Hanley. Green's novel *Living* (1929) is a sensitive evocation of the lives of iron foundry workers in Bridesley, Birmingham, in the late twenties. A lyrical, curiously beautiful book, *Living* recreates the day-to-day lives of Mr Craighan, an ageing moulder, and those who share his home, including his helper, Jim Dale, a workmate named Joe Gates and his daughter Lily, and Bert Jones, a young worker who marries Lily. It is Jones who typifies the workers, who identifies the causes of worker discontent, and who finally is able to find a way out of the dilemma he and his mates are in. The workers' problems, by now familiar to the reader of working-class fiction, are redefined by Jones in the context of foundry life. One of the most important considerations here is safety, and the workers are unconvinced that the owners are taking proper precautions. In one instance Craighan suffers a near fatal accident because of unsafe equipment, and Jones comments bitterly to Jim Dale: 'Ah, it's a firm ain't it. Twisting, twisting all the time. And by all I 'ear what nearly made your old man a goner was the fault of their never getting new equipment. It's the same old tale ... they don't give you a square deal. If you work for them they ought to see you can do it with a decent amount of safety.' Elsewhere Jones complains of pressure from the works manager, a tyrant the men call ''Tis 'im', who never allows them a moment's relaxation. He speaks of an occasion when 'I 'adn't put down the 6 inch file I was using about 20 seconds, just time to blow my nose and the old man ... was all over me and threatens to suspend me. Well that's not treatin' you right. I tell you I'd like to get out of that place.' The desire to get out is underscored by Jones' recognition that there is little hope for change in the foreseeable future: 'Us working people we got to work for our living ... 'til we're too old. It's no manner of use thinking about it, it's like that, right on till we're too old for them to use us.' Unlike many earlier protagonists, however, Bert Jones makes no attempt to change the conditions of working-class life. He follows instead a more selfish path, escaping the unending regimentation of factory life by breaking completely with his milieu, deserting his wife, and emigrating to Canada.

A similar set of conditions, exacerbated by the depression of the thirties, confronts the hero of Walter Greenwood's *Love on the Dole* (1933). But Harry Hardcastle has neither the spirit nor the intelligence of Bert Jones, and is portrayed throughout the novel as a passive victim of economic circumstance. From the beginning his life follows a pattern predetermined by others, at first by those who control the factory complex where he is apprenticed, later by government authorities. At fourteen Harry leaves school to supplement the family income and is apprenticed at Marlowe's, a large engineering works, to learn the operation and maintenance of a range of metal fabricating machines. From that point on he is represented as a typical young worker, his life a series of difficulties and disillusionments. On his first day at work, for example, he is pigeonholed by a resigned older worker, who sees him as 'another recruit to this twelve thousand strong army of men who, all, at one time had come, eagerly, to some such place as this on a similar errand.... All had been young Harrys then. They now were old, disenchanted Harrys; families dependent on their irregular and insufficient wages; no respite to the damnable eternal struggling.' Before long Harry becomes aware that his apprenticeship is merely an arrangement by which the factory owners assure themselves of cheap labour: 'There was no painstaking instruction, no enlightenment of the "mysteries" of the trade as had been promised in the extravagant language of the indentures.' As his friend Larry Meath points out: 'Nobody'll teach you any-thing simply because there's so little to be learnt. You'll pick up all you require by asking questions and watching others work.' After two years Harry is promoted from errand boy to lathe operator. But the pride he takes in his new position is shortlived when he realises its economic consequences. Pre-viously he had received extra money for running special errands, and had shared in the winnings of the older men from racing bets. Now he was one of the men himself, locked in to a pay-packet of ten shillings a week until the end of his indentures. An interlude of freedom is afforded him when he wins £20 on a bet. But a five-day seaside holiday only makes him more aware than ever of his servitude to Hanky Park, the working-class district abutting the factories where he lived: he was 'Hanky Park's prisoner on ticket of leave.' Though he and his girlfriend Helen dream of living else-where, they do nothing about it, submitting without ques-tion to the idea that only locally could they possibly find work: 'in all the wide, wide world Hanky Park was the only place they knew of where they could find someone to buy their labour.'

Things get worse for Harry when his apprenticeship ends. The hope of 'securing a situation on full pay' proves illu-sory, and at twenty-one Harry finds himself on the dole: 'nothing to do with time; nothing to spend; nothing to do tomorrow or the day after; nothing to wear; can't get married. A living corpse; a unit of the spectral army of three million lost men.' His situation is even more bleak when he finds out first that Helen is pregnant and then that he is being thrown off the dole because 'in the opinion of the Public Assistance Committee his father's dole and [his sister] Sally's wages were sufficient to keep him.' Beaten down by the cir-cumstances of his life, Harry can only long 'for a hole to crawl into so that he might relieve himself in bitter tears.' Unable to summon up the working-class hero's traditional sense of defiance against the forces that cause his suffering, he alter-nates between considering suicide and dreaming of the good old days, 'money in pocket . . . and a job to go to on Monday.'

Like his unemployed father, he felt 'the canker of impotence gnaw ... his vitals.' In the end Harry Hardcastle is saved only when his sister becomes the mistress of Sam Grundy, the owner of a chain of betting shops, and through Grundy's influence he is given a permanent job. While such a contrived ending seriously weakens the novel, it may be argued that its very implausibility underscores the hopelessness of Harry's situation and, by extension, that of his peers. This would seem to be Greenwood's intent, for in the final analysis *Love on the Dole* is a 'Condition of the People' novel, designed to illustrate the extent and degree of working-class suffering in the depression, but also to offer comforting reassurance that the workers were submissively accepting their lot and that any threat of a workers' revolution to redress their grievances was remote.

The fiction of James Hanley, particularly the first two novels of his Furys Chronicle (a four novel sequence), offers a different treatment of the working-class hero. In *The Furys* (1935) and *The Secret Journey* (1936) Hanley describes the lives of an Irish family living in a working-class slum squeezed between factories and docks in Gelton (Liverpool) in the twenties. Though the family is dominated by the matriarchal figure of Fanny Fury, one of its most compelling members in these two novels is Desmond, the son who longs for a better life and alienates those around him as he moves to secure it. Brought up in a district that is 'dark and gloomy, a sort of black pit, over which there hung a cloud of smoke, of grease and steam', and influenced by his mother's fierce determination never to give in to *them*, Desmond at first seems destined to champion working-class rights. When the rail men decide to walk off the job in sympathy with striking mine workers, Desmond is one of the prime instigators of the move. At this stage in his life, Desmond believes that 'working men aren't greedy ... [they] only want their rights.' 'Where would you be now', he chides a reluctant workmate, 'but for the rights that working men have won in these last ten years? The Capitalists would have driven you into the gutter.' Later, near the end of *The Furys*, rioting workers clash with mounted police and in the ensuing violence Desmond knocks a policeman from his horse, then 'worked his way over the body of the policeman, caught his raised fist in one hand, and without a moment's hesitation struck with the other. "Swine! swine!" Then he fled.'

By the time the reader encounters him again in *The Secret Journey*, Desmond Fury has parlayed his trade union involvement into a full time job running a small union branch office. Alone in the office, he spends much of his time dreaming of personal advancement: 'it seemed to him that one went up by stages until one either reached secretaryship or was adopted as parliamentary candidate. ... Look where he was today, local delegate, with a better wage than he ever received for slinging a hammer in the Length, an office of his own – and what was more important, able to wear his Sunday clothes on weekdays.' His idol and the object of his envy is the inspector of branch offices, who had left all visible traces of his working-class background behind him. And while Desmond sometimes recalls that the union 'had a purpose – to weld the workers together, so that they would be able to stand up for themselves, ... when the inspector, wearing his Raglan overcoat and carrying a rolled umbrella, came in through the door, purpose went out. There was no longer any purpose, only a sudden quickening of the spirit, a delicious thought that he, Desmond Fury, would one day be in the inspector's place.'

To achieve his dream, Desmond consciously rejects his origins. When his sister Maureen comes to him at the office for help, he reprimands her: 'Oh chuck it, for Christ's sake. It seems to be all the artillery the workers have. Bloody tears. People come here every day, crying, crying their hearts out – aye, crying their guts out. We're used to it.' The *we* that Desmond now sees himself a part of is of course the *them* seen by other members of the working-class as enemies and oppressors. Recognising this, Maureen accuses him being 'a bloody scrounger – a damned impostor, setting yourself up as a champion of working men.' Desmond is unaffected by her remonstrance, however, and his betrayal of his origins is confirmed in a number of other episodes throughout the novel. By the end of the novel he has alienated himself from both friends and family, who are fed up with his pretensions and his failure to use his position to help other workers, and who see his current plan of 'putting up for the Gelton Council' as serving a purely selfish ambition.

The tradition within which the working-class hero operates is characterised by two basic attitudes: on the one hand there is a strong sense of class solidarity, on the other a hostility, manifested in a number of ways, towards those who are thought to treat the working man unjustly. In such a tradition the calculated defection of Desmond Fury to *their* camp is an anomaly. Although a number of protagonists within the tradition decide that the fight to redress working-class grievances is not worth carrying on, and for one reason or another give it up, for most of them it is a lifelong commitment. This is the case with the working-class heroes of Alan Sillitoe. Sillitoe's early heroes, the Seaton brothers in *Saturday Night and Sunday Morning* and *Key to the Door*, Smith in The Loneliness of the Long-Distance Runner and the protagonists in later stories in that volume as well as those in *The Ragman's Daughter*, stand firmly within the tradition established by the industrial novelists of in the 1840's and enriched by those who followed them. Advocating and often participating in violent hostility against the perceived world of *them*, they are motivated by a common set of assumptions and attitudes. Their background is clearly defined; they know who they are and where they come from. Almost from the moment they are introduced to the reader, they are seen to share a highly-developed sense of social awareness. Generally this results in society being viewed as a battleground on which two forces, variously known as *them* and *us*, masters and men, employers and hands, owners and slaves, perpetually confront one another. The continuing ascendency of *them* and what is perceived to be the continuing inequitable distribution of wealth, coupled with the feeling that those who work with their hands should have a greater share of that wealth, normally results in an aggrieved sense of injustice which is translated by most working-class heroes into belligerent language and frequently into violent action. In political terms they share an awareness that leads them to reject the parties which stand for preservation of the social and economic status quo, usually laissez-faire capitalism, and instead espouse the cause of socialism, or in extreme cases the doctrines of anarchism. The attitudes and experiences of Sillitoe's protagonists in the Nottingham fiction echo in many ways those of the working-class heroes who preceded them, suggesting not only that Sillitoe was conscious of the tradition, but that for some time he was satisfied to work comfortably within it. In some of his later fiction, and particularly in *The Death of William Posters* and *A Tree on Fire*, he would test its limits, taking his working-class heroes well away from the slum worlds they would normally inhabit, giving them new roles, and placing them deep in alien territory.

Notes and References

[1] In the interests of readers who might wish to obtain copies of the novels quoted in this chapter, the most widely available editions are listed in the bibliography.
[2] Gissing here echoes Dickens' dislike of union organisers, whom he felt had little genuine sympathy for the individual working man. See *Hard Times*, Book Two, Chapter Four – the confrontation between Slackbridge and Stephen Blackpool.

Chapter Nine

Out of the Ghetto:

The Working-class Hero
in *The Death of William Posters*
and *A Tree on Fire*

In 1965, fourteen years after he had left Nottingham for good, Alan Sillitoe published his fourth novel, *The Death of William Posters*. Although it was not apparent to reviewers at the time, the novel was the first part of a trilogy which follows the development of a Nottingham factory worker as he moves out of the familiar surroundings of his working-class environment and into a world of wider physical and spiritual horizons. With the publication two years later of a second novel in the series, entitled *A Tree on Fire*, the pattern became clear. Together the two novels form a continuing and essentially complete chronology of the politicising of Frank Dawley, a twenty-seven-year-old machine repairman who has become deeply dissatisfied, not only with his place in society but also with his own long-standing passive acceptance of it. (Although Dawley appears prominently in the final novel of the trilogy, *The Flame of Life* (1974), his character is not appreciably altered from the stage reached at the end of *A Tree on Fire*.) Faced with a burning need to find answers to questions that are at once personal and political, Dawley leaves his job, wife and children and embarks on a pilgrimage which takes him first into troubling confrontation with the values of middle-class England and finally into actual combat as a guerilla fighter in the Algerian war of independence. Yet the link with Nottingham remains strong. No matter how extended Dawley's forays into alien territory, both at home and abroad, his working-class background is a constant companion. Although his limited Nottingham environment of home, factory and pub is seen only in flashbacks in both novels, its imperatives continue to condition his outlook and his actions.

It is not surprising, then, that perceptive critics attempted to define Dawley in terms of earlier Sillitoe heroes with whom he shared a common background. Frank Kermode, reviewing *The Death of William Posters* for the *New Statesman*, saw the hero in the mould of the Seatons, still 'potent, belligerent . . . victimised but independent' yet 'ageing a little from book to book.'[1] Bernard Lockwood, in an unpublished dissertation, found him to be 'in a direct line of descent from . . . earlier rebel-protagonists . . . belligerently opposed to the Establishment' in the manner of Arthur Seaton and of Smith. Paul Levine, writing in the *Hudson Review*, came nearer the mark when he called Dawley 'a somewhat older but still unreconciled Arthur Seaton', an assessment which is confirmed in another unpublished dissertation by J. W. Burns, which cites Sillitoe's assertion in an interview that his 'intention was to show the political awakening and development of an Arthur Seaton.' In fact, when Sillitoe was working on the original draft of *The Death of William Posters* he did not settle on a name for his hero until he had written over a hundred pages of the manuscript: in the meantime he called him Arthur Seaton.[2]

An awareness of this close relationship between Frank Dawley and Sillitoe's first protagonist is of some importance, for it clearly attests to the continuing presence of strongly-held working-class attitudes and assumptions in the first two novels of the trilogy. Yet the crucial question for critical readers is whether Sillitoe has been able to fashion a hero who can build on and modify conventional working-class wisdom to help him shape a meaningful life outside the slums. At first glance this would seem unlikely. Despite the fact that he has had a decade to mature and develop, Dawley subscribes to viewpoints that are remarkably close to those of younger protagonists in the earlier fiction. Working-class awareness of a *them–us* dichotomy, for example, a focal point for the thoughts of Sillitoe's earlier heroes, conditions Frank's outlook as well. Members of the middle-class who snub him are 'unsociable bastards' and the upper classes 'bray' like asses (DWP: 172, 254). *They* expect the workers to keep to their place, 'to watch the telly or have a few drinks and not be bothered' (32). In an encounter with a rural landowner Dawley is ordered off a private road and feels he is being put upon because the landowner 'smelt fifteen years of overalls on my back' (66). Later he confronts the estranged husband of Pat Shipley, a middle-class nurse with whom he has been living in a small Lincolnshire village after leaving Nottingham, and mocks the smoothness of the man's office-worker hands. Echoing the diatribes of earlier protagonists against those whose lives they feel are made easy by the sweat of the workers, Dawley tells him: 'The world's top heavy with you and your sort who wank people's brains off every night with telly advertisements that make them happy at carrying slugs like you on their backs, but I'd like to see you do a real day's work, if you could' (146). Traditional working-class prejudice against the police, found frequently in the earlier fiction, is also to be found here in Dawley's fantasy on leaving Nottingham and 'the black care of a working life' that the car he had been given a lift in would be stopped by 'a flashing light' with 'a copper's voice on the beam-end of it barking for his passport and licence and laughing in his face that it was too good to last' (10). In the manner of earlier protagonists Dawley also makes a point of condemning the class-conscious British army: 'It's no good being in khaki and having to jump out of your dreams every time some bloke with two pips on his bony shoulder opens his plumby mouth. I know. Was in myself once' (21). And echoing the sentiments of the Seatons, Smith, Liza Atkin and others in the earlier fiction, Dawley makes a number of derogatory remarks about England itself, calling it a little country like 'a bit of eagle-crap dropped out of the sky' having 'that arse-rag, the Union Jack' as its emblem, and needing its 'whole way of life change[d] through some political switch' (passim).

Despite this allegiance to the more conventional assumptions of working-class life voiced by his predecessors, Frank Dawley differs from them in one significant respect: he recognises a need to leave the working-class milieu in order to make sense of his life. The distinction is an important one, for it points to Sillitoe's widening range of subject matter and his controlled, deliberate move away from a dependence on purely working-class experience without rejecting the real world and substituting a framework of abstraction and fantasy, as he had done in *The General*. Dawley's conception of his problem centres on a mythical figure he calls William Posters, named after the signs found everywhere in England on empty walls and vacant shop windows, 'Bill Posters Will Be Prosecuted'. 'All through the twelve years of his factory days and the years of his marriage he had brooded and built up the Bill Posters legend, endowing the slovenly Bill with the typical mentality of the workman-underdog, the put-upon dreg whose spiritual attributes he had been soaked and bombarded with all through his school, home and working life' (16). Clearly following in the tradition of Tressell's ragged-trousered philanthropists, Posters and his like submit, usually passively, to the oppression of their 'betters'. Such masochistic meekness is symbolised for Dawley in the acceptance by his father of the unwritten rules of a working man's club: 'No politics, lads, and no religion. Just drink your pints and sling your darts, heads down for Bingo and look alive to win a fiver at the end. When you're off sick, we'll look after you, lad, give you a bit of club money, like, and a seaside booze-up once a year. But ... don't think ... You're all free as long as you do as you're told' (73).

Dawley becomes obsessed with the image of Posters, which 'hung around him like a piteous and dying dog' (16). In vain he tries to invest him with mythic stature, picturing him as the historical representative of working-class rebellion against overbearing authority figures:

Bill has been infamous in these streets for generations, bandit Posters, as well known or maybe scorned and scoffed at as Robin Hood, justly celebrated in that hundred verse 'Ballad of Bill Posters' recited for generations in Nottingham streets and pubs. . . . His existence explains many puzzles. Who was General Ludd? None other than the shadowy William Posters, stockinger, leading on his gallant companies of Nottingham lads to smash all that machinery. . . . Who set fire to Nottingham Castle during the Chartist riots? Later, who spat in Lord Roberts' face when he led the victory parade in Nottingham after the Boer War? Who looted those shops in the General Strike? No one has ever proved it, but the ballad sings of it, and historians may make notes for future conjectures (17–18).

The historical fantasy only convinces him that Posters is a master of cunning and evasiveness, however, which does little to alter his original conception of him as the type of workman who believed 'that since something in life was unattainable you had to stop reaching for it, that it was better to rot among the slums and ruins of a played-out way of life, persecuted and prosecuted', than to strive for equality and justice (311). But although the attitude Posters represents remains unacceptable to Dawley, he still finds it 'difficult to get rid of him [and his code of values] precisely because his sympathies were in the right place, and because the conditions that made Bill Posters still persisted' (16). There can be little disagreement with Frank Kermode's assertion that Bill Posters is 'an agreeable invention', for in using it Sillitoe is able to provide his hero with a legitimate, if somewhat contrived, motivation for leaving Nottingham. Unable to accept the assumptions which govern Posters' behaviour, yet sympathetic to his predicament, Dawley is faced with a dilemma which can only be resolved outside the limiting confines of the working-class ghetto.

His odyssey begins in the Lincolnshire village where he settles in to live with Pat Shipley, a middle-class conservative. In a series of long conversations with her, he attempts to explain his need to escape the crushing boredom of what Frank McGuinness in the *London Magazine* called 'his role as one more wage-slave of Britain's industrial machine'. In response to her claim that 'the natural order of things works pretty well', for example, he contends that his 'mates' were almost all unhappy with the status quo, 'working in oil and noise, and then going home at night to a plate of sawdust sausages and cardboard beans' with television 'advertisements telling them that those sausages and beans burning their guts are the best food in the country' (44). Pointing out that his fellow workers are fed up being 'treated like cretins', he argues that among them 'there was a collective wish to change the way things are run, so that they'll have the power of running things. If that happened it wouldn't be a treadmill anymore. They wouldn't strike. They'd be too busy. And too interested in running it' (44). Such conversations serve a useful purpose, for through them Dawley learns to articulate his position, however idealistic it may be. And he learns to think of social reform, as Allen Penner points out in his critical study entitled *Alan Sillitoe*, 'as an endeavour which could give his life meaning and direction.' Yet the longer he stays with Pat he more he experiences a growing sense of rootlessness, of 'not knowing where he belonged' (98). Unable to call on the past for guidance because 'there's no Adam and Eve in our sort of family', and unsure of the future to the point where he felt drawn to old newspapers lying on the floor 'as if one might contain the message of his life', he spends much of his time reading books from Pat's well-stocked library (68, 112). Unlike the heroes of earlier novels (with the qualified exception of Brian Seaton), Frank Dawley reads voraciously, caught up by the novelty of the experience and spurred on by his newfound consciousness that 'such continual reading was altering the basic mechanism of his senses' (92). The process of self-education is interrupted, however, when he resorts to physical violence in a heated argument. Pat, ashamed and enraged because 'this final end to a quarrel had never been imposed on her before', responds by mocking his working-class mores: 'If you want to do that you can get back to your housing estate or slum. I suppose they love it there' (102). The eruption of class antagonism signals the end of the relationship, and after a further violent outbreak follows the appearance of Pat's estranged husband Keith, Dawley leaves abruptly for London.

In the second section of the novel Dawley finds work as a Soho car park attendant and continues to educate himself through selective reading, 'concentrating on English social history of the nineteenth century to find some explanation for the world he had grown up in' (219). As his critical faculties develop he begins to consider alternatives to the passive acceptance of social injustice by Posters and those like him. Convinced by now that he had left home because 'pessimism is an idleness inside you, a spiritual deadness' which has to be replaced with positive action, he begins to believe that 'people can act' to change the world if they feel strongly enough about it (196, 217). (Though the idea may seem thoroughly shopworn to some readers, it is nonetheless appropriate to the circumstances in which Dawley finds himself at this stage in the novel.) He also comes to see himself as a socialist, and he speculates tentatively on an ideal society in which the most important value would be work. These deliberations are encouraged by his growing friendship with Myra Bassingfield, a young matron on the verge of revolt against the hollowness of a life in which she 'bottled, smoked, salted, pickled, baked and pre-packed; collected cook books and recipes from the *Observer* and *Sunday Times*, wrote cheques for magazines pandering to house and home, namely *Which? Where? How? When?* and *What?* [and felt herself becoming] a super householder driven into the ground by it' (169). Convinced by Dawley that the way to a more meaningful existence lies in a dramatic break with her present way of life, and by his assertion that 'it's not what people are that matters; it's what they want to become', Myra leaves her husband (238). Together they make their way to Majorca, driven by Dawley's growing conviction that 'my life and this big island are [too] meshed up and I've got to separate them' (233).

In the third and final section of the novel Frank Dawley's random observations on the nature of society become more coherent. Under the tutelage of Shelley Jones, an American gun-runner, he is introduced to the idea of direct participation in revolutionary activity. In their first conversation, after a fortuitous meeting on the ferry to Majorca, Shelley suggests that workers like Dawley would probably have fought for the Republicans in the Spanish Civil War. Dawley's reaction, to the effect that workers in England in the thirties were too busy worrying about where their own next meal was coming from to consider helping others, prompts Shelley to ask what it is that Frank, the disaffected worker, is looking for now. His answer, 'a world to build, maybe', causes Shelley to respond: 'Fine, pal. But you got to pull down a few first' (253). Dawley's reply, 'I don't mind starting that way', suggests that he has already taken an important step in ridding himself of the Posters ethos. Though it is 'a rather sterile philosophy...that of the necessity to destroy', as J. W. Burns has pointed out, it is also a predictable response at this stage in Dawley's development. His agreement does not commit him to personal involvement in revolutionary activity, it simply indicates his willingness to accept the possibility of participation. At this point he is still groping, considering the alternatives his reading and experience have suggested. This becomes clear in his conversation with a friend of Myra's a short time later. In response to being called 'the Uncomplicated Person', Dawley calls himself 'the empty man, the man without religion. All I believe in is houses and factories, food and power-stations, bridges and coalmines... [and] turning millions of things out on a machine that people can use' (259). Selecting other images such as a hammer and a railway, he adumbrates 'a whole landscape of industrial and material necessity' with which the 'new men' of the world, 'people who think like me', are going to have to come to terms (260). The contradictory urges to build and to destroy exist side by side for Dawley at this point, the former an idealistic dream of a brave new world run by and for the workers, the latter a possible method of achieving it.

As Dawley moves restlessly with Myra from Majorca to Granada and then to Morocco, his thoughts focus increasingly on the need for some kind of positive action as a way of separating himself from the 'world of moribund William Posters' (272). Hell, he has come to believe, is 'the inability to work, to act, to do'; it is also 'having nothing to live for' (272). The opportunity to act is provided when Dawley again encounters Shelley Jones, who is running weapons to insurgents fighting in the Algerian war of independence. When Shelley asks for his assistance on the next run, 'Frank said yes after a bare minute of packed thought' that he planned to 'sort out' later (288). Though the decision is taken quickly, it is nonetheless a logical extension of Dawley's earlier resolves, and his subsequent deliberations – his 'sorting out' of the decision – make this clear. In the tradition of other working-class heroes who recognise the importance of work and who share a commitment to help others less fortunate than themselves, Dawley concludes that 'there's no such thing as happiness except when you are doing work for yourself that at the same time is helping other people' (286). He also sees a 'natural connection' between his life as a factory worker and his present role as a worker in the cause of Algerian independence (293). In both instances he can see himself as one of *us*, a member of a victimised group almost instinctively antipathetic to their oppressors. He now feels ready to participate in a concerted attack against *them* with some prospect of success, and in doing so he can kill off the inhibiting image of 'that snivelling muffle-capped man on the eternal run who'd never had a Bren at his shoulder', William Posters (311). In the novel's final pages Dawley commits himself fully to the cause of insurrection, resolving to leave Myra, who is now pregnant, in Tangiers while he joins forces with the Algerian insurgents. As the gun-runners' truck loaded with arms and ammunition moves out into the desert, he recognises that his journey is a pilgrimage of liberation in more than one sense, offering the possibility of continued spiritual growth as he becomes 'reconstituted' in his passage through the desert wasteland (318).

Although *The Death of William Posters* is open-ended, with Frank Dawley's final development yet to be recorded, Sillitoe has by its close allowed his hero to take a giant step forward on the road to self-discovery without losing touch with his working-class origins. In doing so Sillitoe continued to be guided by critical precepts he formulated some years earlier and expressed in the *TLS* and elsewhere, namely that the writer's role is to reflect contemporary social injustice, to be committed to the improvement of society, and that the ideal perspective for such a writer is a working-class one. It is a measure of Sillitoe's growth as a writer that in *The Death of William Posters* this perspective is no longer circumscribed by the confined milieu of back-to-backs and factories, but is brought to bear on experience gained in a wider world. A similar situation occurs in *A Tree on Fire*, the second novel of the trilogy, published in 1967.

As the novel opens, Frank Dawley moves slowly across the desert in a north-easterly direction from the Moroccan frontier with a small guerilla patrol of the Algerian Front de Libération Nationale (FLN). The eventual goal of the patrol is to rendezvous with other insurgents near the Mediterranean to attack a major French airfield. In the meantime there is constant danger of death from enemy forces and from the severity of nature as well. Dawley's apprehension of the desert, like his perception of so many aspects of 'this ideological adventure', is coloured and made less formidable through reference to his Nottingham background (TF: 158). The burning wilderness of sand dunes, for example, evokes 'the slaghills of Nottinghamshire multiplied a thousand times as far as the eye could see, humps and pyramids of grey dust and shale covering the plain, not so geometrically pure and satisfying as those in the wayback of home but something to draw in the breath at and wonder if this was to be your last sight on earth' (159). When he is vexed considering how 'the mind [can] live when you must learn to walk without hoping to get anywhere, never a point or picture set at or beyond the horizon on which you can visualise and feed', he resolves to 'match it with what life had been like when he was in the factory' (162). Thoughts of his earlier life prompt Dawley to remember the long gestation of 'his giant idealisms' (162). He tells Shelley that 'even as a kid I'd had ideas as to what the world should be like and how it should be run', and he recalls the frustration of living in conditions which for 'three generations of family . . . engendered nothing but despair' (162, 166). In the Algerian desert, however, he senses a new beginning, with 'the landmarks . . . unknown and unimaginable so that one could hope . . . and the joy of it was in his head' (162). Aware that 'life had so far trained him to deal with the world [only] in simple and mechanical terms', he feels exhilarated as the prospect of 'desert trek and loneliness brought reflection' (174).

As Dawley does reflect, examining his motives for joining the FLN, he is by turns idealistic and selfish. On the one hand he convinces himself that 'he had wanted to fight so that those considered the exploited and down-trodden could stand up to the so-called master races of Europe' (216). This commitment to violent confrontation with *them* is strengthened when the French bomb and nearly obliterate a village in which the guerillas have stopped to rest, for he finds in the attack 'one big answer to keep me going. . . . *They* can't do this all the time and get away with it' (177).[3] Dawley's outraged cry from 'the black kingdom of Downtroddendom' is fuelled both by memories of social injustice in England and by a dream of post-revolutionary Algeria in which the desert will be transformed by 'ice-factories and water-pumps, power stations and fish-pools, cotton farms and air-conditioned mills, soil labs and canning-plants' run by the workers for their own benefit (154). On the other hand, he recognises that his motives are not always altruistic, that 'you worked with those at the bottom in order to be reborn' (178). When asked by a young insurgent why he had come to Algeria, he answers: 'I came to help people who needed help', but he is quick to add: 'and to help myself' (367). For Dawley, and for the reader as well, it becomes increasingly difficult to separate personal and political quests. The confusion is perhaps inevitable in the kind of socially conscious fiction Sillitoe was writing early in his career, for he was unwilling to let his protagonist discard one of the central biases of working-class culture, the view of society as a battleground between *them* and *us*. In doing so, of course, he ran the risk that the reader would see the protagonist as merely a type, a kind of super-socialist preaching the gospel of a new heaven on earth. At times it seems that this is about to happen, when, for example, Dawley employs religious rhetoric to describe guerilla action in which 'his rifle or machine-gun joined the chorus of others, the new gunchurch of the revolution spitting out their cleansing hymns' (209). A similar feeling is invoked when he finds an analogy for his present role as armed insurgent and his earlier role as factory worker:

> to comprehend perfectly all details of a complex plan, and at the same time to know that he was taking part in it, filled him with a transcendental joy and gave meaning to his existence. He was again united with the only part of the world that mattered. It was a similar experience, certainly as real and perhaps more valuable, to when he was first set on a machine in the factory fifteen years ago. The great lathe was fixed before him, and when the tool-setter showed the blueprint of what was to be made on it and then produced one as an example, he understood the plan, the object, and its purpose in the lorry-engine for which it was due. He was making something useful, and there was no deeper satisfaction, until he chafed at the fact that there was an even greater pattern to strive for and fit his life into (226).

It would be easy enough to read the 'greater pattern' which circumscribes Dawley's present activity as 'the working class in its struggle to establish equality, brotherhood and justice on earth.'[4]

Despite the ease with which Frank Dawley may be fitted into a pattern and seen with some legitimacy as a vehicle for political propaganda, he remains a credible, individualised character rather than a type. His passionate involvement with Pat Shipley, his love for Myra, and his deep personal regard for Shelley all mark him as a man who cares for particular individuals and not only for the suffering masses. His reaction to the grimmer aspects of an insurgent's life reveals his deep humanity, as the searing immediacy of the following passage illustrates:

> They dragged the bodies behind the rocks, and swept dust over the tracks and pools of blood.... He turned from the dead young men, his heart bursting. He was familiar with the dead, but the more he saw, the more depressed he was. He supposed the war would go on until one side or another lost heart, felt the shadow only of so much useless death, instead of pure energy-giving rage at the stony manifestation of another row of corpses. Slogans, ideals and beliefs weakened when you pulled the warm bodies towards the holes you had lain in while waiting to kill them, with their tortured faces and limbs still jumping. He took all field-dressings from their packs before heaping on the stones (211).

Earlier Sillitoe heroes were not permitted the release of tears; indeed they were seldom in a position in which tears would have been appropriate. But they are the measure of Dawley's agony on more than one occasion, allowing him a 'pouring out of sorrow and loneliness, heartache and despair' (221). One can find numerous other incidents to substantiate Dawley's individuality throughout *The Death of William Posters* and *A Tree on Fire*, demonstrating that he is neither an automaton nor a mere puppet made to dance a political jig. Rather, his political activities in Algeria should be seen as the culmination of a personal quest which began when he left the Nottingham slums. In the process of rejecting some key assumptions of working-class life, and in particular in ridding himself of Bill Posters, he comes to see the desirability of individual involvement to alter a world in which

Posters' philosophy of despair has been allowed to flourish unchecked. Assisting Shelley in delivering guns to Algerian insurgents and later joining the FLN, Frank Dawley creates a role for himself that is at once personally fulfilling and in his own terms politically justifiable.

The fusing of Dawley's personal and political quests is both explicable and appropriate, for in *The Death of William Posters* and *A Tree on Fire* Sillitoe is working within and extending the convention of the working-class hero in fiction, chronicling hitherto unexplored aspects of the long-established tradition of working-class antipathy against *them*. The typical working-class hero had been primarily, though not only, a representative of his class, a spokesman for class grievances and class loyalties. In the first two novels of Sillitoe's trilogy those grievances and loyalties are expanded to encompass the suffering of 'a country labouring under barbarous torments and oppression' (156). Within the tradition Frank Dawley may be seen as the first working-class hero to transcend the slum environment, modifying and building on conventional working-class wisdom to shape a meaningful life outside the confines of the ghetto. At the end of *A Tree on Fire*, after the planned attack on the airfield has taken place, Dawley contracts a serious illness. For ten days he lies feverish and unconscious in a village hut and is then transferred to an FLN field hospital to convalesce. Carefully evaluating his position as he slowly recuperates, and realising that his immediate usefulness as a guerilla fighter is over, he decides to return to England to raise money for the insurgents' cause. After a brief visit to Nottingham, he sets out to join Myra and to see the son she has borne him. Finding that her large home is now shared by the friend who brought them together, Albert Handley, along with Handley's unpredictable family, Dawley decides to stay.

To make sense of Frank's decision one must examine the forceful personality of Albert Handley, a character which John Coleman in the *Observer* called 'a formidable comic creation' and the *London Magazine* reviewer saw as 'a splendidly original figure.' Handley is a middle-aged eccentric painter, in some ways like Cary's Gulley Jimson, who lives and works in a large rundown house in the Lincolnshire countryside with his wife Enid, seven children, his brother John and a bulldog named Eric Bloodaxe. When he first meets Dawley in a pub near Pat Shipley's cottage, he has not yet been discovered by the art world and supports his family by raffling pictures to neighbours and acquaintances (but never giving away a prize) and sending begging letters to notables whose names he has culled from *Who's Who*. The two men have much in common, including their working-class upbringing in Midlands industrial cities, working experience in factories, and a number of shared attitudes and assumptions about life. Handley, who sees himself as 'an artist and an anarchist', is predictably anti-establishment and anti-authoritarian, and like other early Sillitoe hero-figures believes that 'there's nothing like violent change to shake perspective into place' (19, 98). He has no time for patriotic feelings, and refers to England as 'the maggoty homeland' (337). He is against monarchy, the established church, landlords and 'toffee-nosed posh papers' (45). And in the tradition of working-class antipathy directed towards *them*, he blusters against government representatives such as customs men with 'servile snuffed-out porridge faces', and boasts of the many times he has cunningly removed his watch 'before walking into the National Assistance Board' (13, 21). Once his work becomes known and his financial worries disappear, he finds other targets to shoot at, but the rhetoric of class antagonism remains. His 'real enemies' are now art critics and editors, whom he sees as 'queers, frauds, playboys or brainless public school sacks of blood' (DWP: 212). To Handley they are all parasites living off 'people who are trying to do real work', and he dreams of a time when he can 'stand them up against a wall and shoot them down' (DWP: 209, TF: 45).

Handley sees himself as 'a revolutionary by faith', and he makes a distinction between his own intense commitment to the concept and the lip-service paid to it by 'those middle-class English marxists who live in Hampstead or the juiciest of Home Counties, because at the first sniff of civil strife they'd join the government militia or run to hide in the nearest police station' (TF: 308-9). Because he believes that the present social system should 'support us while we're trying to bring it crashing down', he invests a substantial sum in industrial shares and uses the dividends to help 'any trouble-making or revolutionary organisation aimed at disrupting the system we live under' (36, 446). He also supports his brother John, a mentally ill ex-prisoner-of-war who had given 'secret lectures on militarism and the class war' in a Japanese concentration camp and now prepares for 'the great hundred years' war against imperialism and the established order, class war, civil war, dark and light war, the eternal conflict of them against us and us against them' (42, 322). Handley's sons Adam and Richard, whom John has educated 'from the age of five in the romance and ethics of revolution, in the mechanics of insurrection', are encouraged to spend their time printing and distributing leaflets and conducting a series of elaborate war games (290-91). For a time Handley even has hopes that another son, Cuthbert, will soon 'have infiltrated right into the middle of the enemy's juiciest pie' by 'becoming an ordained priest in the Church-of-England' (444). His commitment to revolution is rounded off by turning his house into an arsenal, well stocked with guns and food, ready to withstand a prolonged siege should a battle with government forces come about.

The reader might dismiss much of this as romantic indulgence on Handley's part if it were not for the fact that he clear-sightedly realises that civil or class war is unlikely to come about quickly because England, with its 'peculiar self-satisfied ... pipe-smoking resignation', 'lacks the imagination or energy to be revolutionary' (109, 279). Handley is no fool, and maintaining the infrastructure of revolution around him serves an important purpose in his life. To understand this one must recognise that Handley, with 'his demanding visions' is more than anything else an artist (289). He lives largely in 'the endless world of his work that he was king of and could walk across at will, that dominated all waking and sleeping hours as if life and sanity depended on it. Reaching beyond the end of what he had never seen any other artist do, he was out in the wilderness, crawling through fire with an unquiet soul' (46). In the context of his art, revolution may be seen to have a two-fold meaning. On the one hand 'the idea of revolution' acts as a spur to the creative imagination, providing the 'spiritual energy' needed for the production of his work. The hoped for result is original and compelling art with the power to 'get you by the scruff of the neck and pull you into either bathroom or jungle and show you things you'd never seen because you'd been afraid you might like the horror of them' (336). On the other hand it allows him to remain independent of pressures to produce art which fails to disturb. His professional creed is simply stated: 'You can be a successful shop-keeper or football player or film-maker or critic, but you can never be a successful artist. As soon as you succeed you fail' (257). Handley's formula for guarding against such 'success' is to adopt a revolutionary stance: 'You can't live at peace with the world. Not this world which won't ever let you live at peace with it except on its own impossible strait-jacket terms.... The world hasn't got to be only lived in, because even if you keep yourself at a distance it will corrupt and destroy you by forcing you to keep your distance, but it has to be continually attacked, raided, sabotaged, marauded, plundered, insulted and spat on.... You only make your mark and set up your score by giving no quarter either within or beyond the law' (442). The infrastructure of revolutionary activity with which he surrounds himself supports this stance and at the same time acts as a reminder of his working-class sympathies.

Handley's dual allegiance to his class and to his art leads him to the conclusion that 'revolution is the only remaining road of spiritual advance' (308). It is a thesis that can be easily accepted by Frank Dawley, who shares his dedication to the creation of a better world. As the novel ends he joins forces with Handley's 'talented and bandit crew, *franc-tireurs* of the atomic and conformist age', and looks forward to 'years of invigorating chaos ahead, of great ideas, and great work' (433, 447). For Dawley, returning to English soil to begin a new offensive by raising funds for the insurgents' cause, the wheel has come full circle. Conditioned and prepared for life in a working-class milieu, he has examined the central assumptions of that milieu and adapted them to suit his own needs. At the same time he has found in the working-class sense of social injustice the seeds of a reformist creed that has led to political activism and given a direction to his life. Having gone through a literal baptism of fire in the front lines of guerilla warfare in Algeria, he returns to his homeland to take up a new life as a crusader for far-reaching social change.

Insistence on the need for dramatic social upheaval has been a consistent theme in Sillitoe's work since *Saturday Night and Sunday Morning*, but earlier heroes, drawn at different stages of maturity, were not allowed a total commitment to the cause. Although there is a limited involvement in subversive activity by the protagonists of *Saturday Night and Sunday Morning*, *The Loneliness of the Long-Distance Runner* and *Key to the Door*, their rebellious gestures at times reflect as much a muscle-flexing egotism as a desire to reform a corrupt society. In *The Death of William Posters* and *A Tree on Fire*, however, Sillitoe's protagonist reaches new levels of awareness and personal commitment which lead, as Allen Penner has pointed out, to a 'self-effacing and beneficent dedication to the common good.' Yet this has been achieved without compromising the *them–us* philosophy espoused by earlier heroes. As Penner observes, Dawley 'loves his fellow revolutionaries and the economically deprived, but he still hates passionately "the haves". Sillitoe has altered the dedication of his hero, but he has kept intact the old animosities.' The working-class ethos remains strong.

The publication of *The Ragman's Daughter* in 1963 may now be seen to have heralded the end of Sillitoe's exclusive reliance on the difficult conditions of English urban working-class life to sustain the social criticism of his heroes. It is the mark of his resilience that in the first two novels of the trilogy the reformist impulse engendered in two men of working-class stock by their sense of social injustice is applied in quite different circumstances. Frank Dawley is motivated to contend with repression of the Algerian desire for independence and to join an insurrectionary movement in the north African desert. Albert Handley uses the idea of revolution to stimulate the creation of provocative art to combat the forces of social conformity and complacency. In both cases Sillitoe broke new ground while remaining true to the imperatives of the working-class world his earlier works explore and to his own critical principles. Taken together, *The Death of William Posters* and *A Tree on Fire* mark a transition in Sillitoe's writing, in which he moves away from reliance on the scenes from provincial working-class life that dominated his earlier work, and into new settings and the exploration of fresh ways to analyse the complex relationships of men and women in contemporary English society.

Notes and References

[1] Reviews quoted in this chapter are listed in the bibliography.
[2] Information supplied to the author by Alan Sillitoe in an interview at London, August 26, 1968.
[3] Author's italics.
[4] Charles I. Glicksberg, *The Self in Modern Literature*, p. 159.

Chapter Ten

New Directions:

A Survey of Recent Work

The General, a parable of conflicting moral claims in an imaginary wartime setting, was published in 1960, and in the context of Sillitoe's other early fiction it was for some time considered an aberration. Nearly twenty years later it appears in a different light, showing that even in the early years of his career Sillitoe's literary aspirations went beyond providing a chronicle of life in working-class Nottingham. Set in an unlocated place sometime in the present century, it rests on the unlikely premise that a train carrying members of a symphony orchestra to entertain troops at the front has crossed through the lines unmolested and moved freely into enemy territory. Capture is inevitable, and the musicians are condemned to be shot until an enemy general counters the order from High Command and stays the execution in return for the orchestra's promise to play for him. In the event they present Tchaikovsky's Sixth Symphony (the Pathétique), and although the choice is singularly appropriate, the concert itself is almost irrelevant. What concerns both the musicians and the general is the sudden relevance of abstract problems such as the scope for individual action in a world dominated by impersonal forces and imperatives imposed by some unseen authority. At times the entire situation seems unreal, or more appropriately, surreal, given the clinical clarity with which actions and surroundings are described. But for the general and for the orchestra's spokesman, Evart, the problems are real enough as they struggle to reconcile individual needs and political necessities. The novel ends on an ambiguous note concerning the fate of both central characters, and what resolution there is is hedged round by uncertainties. In any case, the barebones of event are of little consequence in this short novel, and it is also arguable that the philosophical issues are approached too tentatively to have much appeal for the seasoned reader. Nonetheless, *The General* remains a valuable indicator of Sillitoe's early interest in and ability to come to grips with problems which clearly transcend the working-class ghetto.

The shift in emphasis away from class-conscious interests in Sillitoe's best-known early work and towards a less limiting concern with the particular effects of communal pressures on individual personalities had its genesis in *The General* and became more obvious in the first two novels of the trilogy. By the mid-sixties it was evident that Sillitoe recognised the limitations of an interpretation of society which only took into account two hostile groupings, and the work he completed during this period began to reflect that awareness. Although he was not to reject the notion that injustice continued to flourish in contemporary English society, he became more and more concerned with the effects of social and political pressures rather than with their causes and possible remedies. The later work should be seen as a series of explorations, some tentative and some more boldly assured, of the ways in which individuals are directed and controlled by environmental and social influences. According to Jeffrey Simmons, who as Sillitoe's editor at W. H. Allen has closely watched his development for the past twenty years, the recent fiction places a greater emphasis than earlier work on the personal ramifications of suffering that circumstances frequently force upon his characters, and it also reveals a more overt display of compassion towards the characters than was usual in earlier novels and stories.

Something of this 'new' Sillitoe is apparent in the collection of stories published in 1968 under the title *Guzman, Go Home*. Although some of them were written much earlier than others, there is a sense of unity about the stories collected here, with many sharing a sensibility that Barry Callaghan in a review for the Toronto *Telegram* likened to 'the world of the terrified child.'[1] Using Dickens and *Great Expectations* as touchstones, Callaghan recalled how 'Pip and others are continually assaulted, pummelled and pounded by blows and bodies that come from nowhere. Nor is this punishment merited. They are simply defenceless.' In such a world even the adult, like a child, 'is threatened or hit by forces too large to comprehend, too swift to avoid.' Callaghan saw in Sillitoe's stories a similar apprehension of reality, a sentiment shared by *The Times* reviewer, who spoke of 'the lions that chase' Sillitoe's characters into madness and despair. Certainly most of the protagonists in these stories, and many of the other characters as well, are victims of circumstance, though most are tough enough to come to an uneasy acceptance of their situation in the end. The narrator in 'Revenge', the first story in the collection, says that 'love is like childhood – golden to recall', and then reminds us that the anguish so often a part of being in love is often conveniently forgotten. His own failed marriage is finely dissected to reveal the causes and effects that eventually pushed him to seek psychiatric help. But when an unexpected turn of events allows him to hear the doctors joking contemptuously about his case, his combined bitterness and rage give him the energy to cope with the situation and to survive. In 'Canals' the rose-coloured glasses of nostalgia are shattered by a chance meeting between ex-lovers after fifteen years apart, and the way to the future is shadowed and uncertain. In 'The Road' a strained marriage is held together a bit longer by a crisis involving an only child, but the forces of disharmony are only pushed back, not conquered. Other stories explore infidelity and loneliness and the communal and personal pressures that capriciously force people apart and chain them together. The title piece is the finest in the collection, an incisive study of a German war criminal and sometime artist who runs a garage in a Spanish mountain town. While his men repair a broken-down car, he attempts to justify his life to the car's owner, a young Englishman. The story has affinities with *The General*, echoing the novel's commentary on the nature of art and war, but there is an added, almost subliminal, element of horror here as Guzman tells his story in fluent though curiously stilted English. It is certainly one of Sillitoe's most compelling works, powerfully reaffirming the need to accept responsibility for one's actions no matter what easy excuses might be provided by extenuating circumstances.

An entirely different approach to the art of narration is evident in Sillitoe's next major novel, *A Start in Life*, published in 1970. As the publisher's advertisements suggested, the new novel 'spectacularly revived the tradition of the picaresque novel ... that flourished so marvellously in this country in the early eighteenth century.' In the manner of classic picaresque fiction, *A Start in Life* was as much as anything a great deal of fun. For the most part critics were taken by surprise, finding it difficult to reconcile this genial new Sillitoe with the chronicler of working-class grievances they felt they knew rather well. The more discerning among them, however, recognised that one of Sillitoe's most intriguing characteristics as a writer is his unpredictability, and responded positively, sharing the sense of fun that pervades the novel's three hundred and fifty pages. In retrospect it is easy to see the inevitability of Sillitoe attempting a comic novel. He had written a number of times of his great admiration for Fielding and of the powerful effect that Jaroslav Hasek's satiric masterpiece, *The Good Soldier Schweik*, had had on him. And in *The Death of William Posters* he had begun to show an inclination towards self-mockery and the consciously literary spoof.[2] But predictable or not, *A Start in Life* must be considered Sillitoe's most entertaining novel to date. Combining elements of satire, irony, farce, literary parody and a number of other traditional humorous devices, it freed him at last from being stereotyped as 'just' a working-class writer, though as the *TLS* reviewer pointed out, the quality of his Nottingham fiction had invalidated any invidious connotation the term might once have had.

Ironically, much of *A Start in Life* is set in working-class areas of Nottingham: it is the childhood and early teenage environment of the novel's protagonist, Michael Cullen. But now the background is merely incidental, taken for granted by writer and reader alike. The focus of our attention is on the narrator himself. At the age of nineteen he leaves Nottingham for good, escaping from a pregnant girlfriend and the stigma of having been let go from an estate agent's employ because of unethical dealings. As he nurses his ageing and decrepit car towards London, he picks up some of the characters whose lives will profoundly influence his own later on; and in the traditional digressive fashion of the picaresque, each of them has a capsulised life story to tell. Arriving in London just as the car finally disintegrates, the roguish hero embarks on a series of adventures which lead him by turns into the employ of two of the capital's most powerful criminals and, after a brief but glamorous period as an international gold smuggler, into the embrace of the law and a consequent acquaintance with Her Majesty's prisons. In the meantime he has been involved in amorous intrigues with a number of delectable trollops, and in the end settles down with one of them in a country retreat to lead a respectable life, or so it seems. For just as our reactions towards the traditional picaro are invariably ambivalent, so in this novel we are sceptical of the hero's final protestations of repentance.

To see *A Start in Life* as merely the chronicle of a rogue's adventures is to miss its satiric thrust. Demonstrating a studied awareness of the genre's satiric possibilities, Sillitoe peppers the contemporary social landscape with a motley collection of fools and rogues, including pseudo-intellectuals and phoney artists, trendies and reactionaries, arch-criminals and co-operative policemen, pneumatic nymphs and self-styled playboys, dim-witted customs men, grasping estate agents and unstable psychiatrists. There is, of course, more than mere entertainment value attached to such character-types. Although their capacity to amuse or instruct must depend to a great degree on the situations in which we encounter them, their collective satiric significance becomes apparent when we look for a common denominator among them. Like the characters in *Guzman, Go Home* they are victims of circumstance, but here the circumstances are largely of their own making, for without exception they prefer to live in a world of fabrications, fantasies and dreams. It is here, in one demonstration after another of the consequences of self-delusion, that the satire bites. Although in the end a ritual blessing is conferred on the protagonist and those he has chosen to live with him in the country, it does not negate the novel's pointed commentary on the common human folly of failing to confront ourselves directly and honestly.

The commercial and critical success of *A Start in Life* was not repeated with Sillitoe's next novel, entitled *Travels in Nihilon* and published the following year. Many reviewers were lukewarm about the new book's merits, and at least one was particularly harsh in his assessment. Interestingly, the most favourable review appeared in the highly-respected *TLS*. It began at the beginning by explaining that 'Nihilon is, simply, the country in the world which shows the political philosophy of Nihilism at its purest and best and most successful. Cheating and violence are elevated into socially acceptable, indeed necessary, codes of behaviour: every trader must overcharge, every motorist is compelled by law to drink and to promote death on the roads, every news bulletin is presented as "the Lies", and personal love and loyalty are unknown.' In twenty-five years since the establishment of the Nihilonian state few visitors have managed to penetrate the country's well-guarded frontiers, and official propaganda reaching the outside world is either wildly exaggerated or contradictory. Sensing that an authoritative guidebook to this topsy-turvy state would be a best-seller, the senior editor of a large publishing house sends five travellers to Nihilon with orders to compile a guidebook of its social, political and topographical contours. The five – a poet, a specialist in politics and military history, a geographer, an aspiring diplomat and a woman who might also be a journalist, enter the country separately and by different modes of transport, and intend to meet in the capital, Nihilon City. What they fail to bargain on, apart from the upside-down codes of behaviour practised by the inhabitants, is their involvement in an insurrection against President Nil and his regime. But the anti-government forces, who espouse conventional honesty, turn out to be just as unscrupulous as their adversaries, a point the novel's final chapters make abundantly clear. As the *TLS* review concluded, the book's 'message is basically one of light and breezy pessimism about most human political systems, about the corruption of technology by power politics, about individual human greed and insensitivity.'

Along the way to his own (inevitably similar) conclusions, the reader is treated to a series of amusing and occasionally hilarious escapades and madcap adventures as the five aspiring Baedeckers get involved in one brouhaha after another. Satirical and farcical at the same time, the novel ends with one of the most outrageously inventive climaxes in modern fiction. Yet the book is not without flaws, the most obvious of which is the disjointed nature of its presentation. As one critic pointed out, Sillitoe's satiric fantasy-voyage has not one Gulliver but five, and the resulting multiple exposure must inevitably produce a blurred image. By the time the reader has left one traveller behind, and has been exposed in turn to the activities of the other four, he finds it difficult to retune his sensibilities to the first traveller on a subsequent encounter. Although the travellers begin to meet some time before the novel ends, the reader's attention may well have wandered by then, and the novel's impact will have been consequently weakened. It seems unlikely that *Travels in Nihilon* will ever have a large following, but it will continue to be of interest to students of Sillitoe's developing career and to specialists in the different kinds of fiction it represents.

In 1972 Sillitoe published a personal memoir entitled *Raw Material*, and from the beginning it has been a difficult book to classify. On page two Sillitoe calls the book 'an attempt at self-portrait' and on the last page but one, 'a historical novel.' Although the two are not necessarily contradictory, assuming the history being fictionalised is family history, neither is completely accurate as a description of what the book actually succeeds in doing. For *Raw Material* is essentially a book about writing, and what it does is to convey something of the complexity of the writer's task and, more specifically, to isolate and document some of the peculiar elements of one writer's familial and communal ancestry, in order to show why he writes as he does. The book is an attempt to come to grips with the process of writing, to investigate the special relationship between a writer and the accumulation of fact and fantasy in his own background that can be called his raw material.

At first the book assumes a more or less formal pattern: chapters which examine Alan Sillitoe's personal background alternate with chapters exploring the process of writing and the problem of conveying 'truth' in artistic form. By the end of Part One, about half way through the book, the distinction becomes less clear. Recollections of childhood begin to be assimilated into commentary on the writer's craft, in effect producing a demonstration of the process Sillitoe is exploring. Much of Part Two is taken up with a highly charged account of British involvement in the Great War of 1914–18. Using carefully documented military history, buttressed with recollections of his uncles' first-hand experiences in the trenches and supplemented by his own lingering feeling of working-class resentment against those who misuse power and authority, Sillitoe manages to infect the reader with his own sense of shame and bitterness at the stupid mismanagement that resulted in the waste of so many men's lives. The final chapters of the memoir range over more recent family history, offer anecdotes that occasionally shed light on the fiction, and continue to explore the writer's relationship to his craft in highly personal terms. Although it must be admitted that these latter commentaries are uneven, sometimes banal, and at times even contradictory, they are not easily dismissed. Taken together with earlier chapters, they serve to remind us that the serious artist's struggle to shape his raw material into a coherent and meaningful form is neither simple nor easy.

In 1973 Sillitoe published his fourth collection of stories, entitled *Men, Women and Children*. All but one of the nine stories it contained had been completed since the publication of *Guzman, Go Home*, though one of these, 'The Chiker', had been begun ten years earlier. Although most of the stories are set in or near Nottingham, the geographical settings have little to do with the stories' development and equally little to do with the characters' image of themselves. The point is worth emphasising, for it distinguishes Sillitoe's more recent work from earlier fiction in which his characters defined themselves primarily in terms of neighbourhood and class. That is to say, as Sillitoe's talent has matured, he has become less dependent on representative attitudes and conditions as means of defining his characters and more concerned with the individual and personal aspects of problems they are forced to confront. At the same time the new stories are markedly more restrained in tone than many of those in the Nottingham fiction, moving quietly and untheatrically to their pointed conclusions. There is evidence to suggest that Sillitoe himself felt rather strongly that the new stories should be seen in a fresh way, without any preconceptions about their settings influencing the reader's response. In a preface to the collection he pointed out that despite his habitual tendency to represent characters who spend much of their time on a Nottingham 'street-corner or a slum or a housing estate', it should be self-evident that 'the breadth of activity, of movement and suffering, is as intense and deep when undergone by the people on this stage as on any other.' He also argued that individuals were the mainstay of his stories, 'not themes, or incidents, or messages of any kind except ... that people who live and suffer make up the sum totality of anything worth writing about.' The sophisticated reader may wish to pay just as little attention to the proscription against finding messages in the work as he does to Mark Twain's famous warning in *Huckleberry Finn*. Nevertheless, Sillitoe's statement stands as a useful reminder of the shift in emphasis in his recent work away from the earlier dogmatic insistence on the need for a total reconstruction of society and towards a compassionate assessment of personal suffering in a world dominated by forces over which the individual has little hope of control.

Of nine stories in *Men, Women and Children* no less than seven explore loneliness and the pain of love, in which passionate involvements result in heartbreak or unwanted pregnancy, marriages break violently apart, and men, women and children suffer the consequences. Some stories have affinities with those in *Guzman, Go Home*: 'Scenes From the Life of Margaret' contains echoes of 'Canals', and 'The Chiker' might profitably be compared with 'Revenge'. Others break fresh ground. 'Enoch's Two Letters', though built on an improbable coincidence, is a penetrating study of childhood dependencies. 'Pit Strike', a moving account of one man's battle with the forces of injustice, makes a strong social statement without diminishing the reader's interest in the powerful central character. The longest story in the collection, entitled 'Mimic', is presented first, and so good is it that one wishes the collection had been retitled to draw attention to it. 'Mimic' is one of the finest pieces of writing Sillitoe has yet produced, an incisive and spell-binding study of a man who copes with life by mimicking it. Significantly, the nameless mimic understands the nature and value of his talent, both in assessing and avoiding his essential self. Finally, after a harrowing descent into madness, he comes to recognise its limitations as well. The story is divided into two parts separated by the protagonist's period of illness and recovery, and moves from his infancy to the age of thirty-five, when he takes the decision to have done with mimicking. He has painfully come to realise that mimicking life, or even mimicking one's mimicry of life, is ultimately self-defeating. Yet in spite of the growing likelihood of this conclusion, such is Sillitoe's skill here that the reader is kept bound to the story and is even unwilling to force the narrator's pace. There is little doubt that as it becomes better known, 'Mimic' will be recognised as a classic example of the story-teller's art.

Sillitoe's eighth novel, *The Flame of Life*, was published in 1974 and completed the trilogy begun in 1965 with *The Death of*

William Posters. In the new novel the principal characters of the earlier two, including Frank Dawley and Albert Handley, work with others such as Handley's independently-minded sons in an attempt to build a meaningful existence in the utopian community set up at the close of *A Tree on Fire*. Convinced of the corrupt nature of contemporary English society, members of the community reflect on their theoretical opposition to its basic concepts and consider ways to disrupt it. At the same time, however, they are involved in a near constant squabbling with each other over domestic arrangements, marital and sexual rights and the problems of sibling rivalry. As a result, the novel is diffuse and difficult to apprehend. A number of critics shared this view, also suggesting that the novel was burdened with too much theory existing in a vacuum with no significant action, either real or contemplated, to give it point. Others said that it was weakly plotted, showing little sense of direction or purpose. And there were fresh reservations about Sillitoe's style, with objections which had not been heard for some time to awkward constructions, the presence of too many ponderous and 'heavy' passages, and to a hectoring and too obviously didactic tone in the speeches of the principal characters. These general impressions were neatly summed up by Maurice Richardson in the *Observer*, who spoke of the novel's prevailing and 'strange atmosphere of unreality, quite foreign to Alan Sillitoe's best work.'

It is tempting to speculate on the reasons why Sillitoe felt it necessary to return in *The Flame of Life* to a more openly reformist brand of fiction than he had been practising in recent years. One likely explanation is that as a committed professional writer he felt it was his duty to finish what he had begun in offering his readers the first two novels of a projected trilogy. That is to say, he felt bound to complete the third novel, rounding off his examination of the characters and issues developed in the earlier two, even though in some ways it would have to deviate from the direction in which his more recent work had been moving. Under such circumstances, a less experienced or talented writer than

Sillitoe might have produced a much worse book than *The Flame of Life*, for despite its flaws, the novel has value as a relevant commentary on the nature of contemporary society. That said, however, one must still conclude that it is the weakest novel he has published to date.

At the time of writing, Sillitoe's most recent novel is *The Widower's Son*, released in 1976 to the resounding cheers of literary critics. Almost without exception the reviews were laudatory: D. A. N. Jones, writing in the *TLS*, called it a 'powerful and original novel, remarkable not least for its accomplished handling of two very difficult subjects, death and sexual congress'; Nick Totton in the *Spectator* commended the 'texture of the writing', pointing to the novel's ability to function effectively on realistic, metaphysical and allegorical levels; Russell Davies in the *Observer* was impressed by its sense of unity, and in an aside provocatively called it 'a good cure for marital complacency'; and Jeremy Brooks in the *Sunday Times* headed his complimentary review with the words: 'Sillitoe discovers his perfect subject.'

That subject was the life story of William Scorton, trained to see life in military terms from early childhood by his widowed father, a professional artilleryman retired with the rank of sergeant-major. Beginning his own army career as a Boy Soldier, Scorton moves quickly through the ranks to become a gunnery officer in the Royal Artillery by 1939. Early in the war he distinguishes himself as a Fire Observation Officer, co-ordinating firepower from extremely hazardous positions during the retreat to Dunkirk, and by war's end has become a colonel. Soon afterwards he marries Georgina, the daughter of a brigadier, and begins to find out that there is a great deal more to life than the army had taught him. As Julian Moynahan pointed out in the *New York Times Book Review*, 'their marriage over ten years develops the character of a military deadlock: each mounts campaigns against the citadel of the other's heart, but always fails because of tactical errors, the strength of the other's resistance, and insufficient knowledge of the place to be stormed and taken.' The marriage slowly crumbles, and with it Scorton's confidence. In the meantime he has left the army and become the manager of a leisure centre, commanding lines of bowling alleys and bingo tables instead of rows of gun emplacements. The abrupt alteration of his lifestyle, openly resented by Georgina, does little for his sense of self-worth, and exacerbates their marital discord. Faced with a rapidly escalating domestic conflict and haunted by the prospect of his wife's infidelity, Scorton suffers a mental breakdown and attempts suicide. This harrowing emotional crisis, which Sillitoe explores in devastating detail, brings Scorton eventually to the beginnings of meaningful self-awareness which neither his father nor the army nor marriage had given him. Alone at the age of fifty, he prepares to begin life again.

With *The Widower's Son* Sillitoe has moved into the mainstream of English fiction. As Moynahan perceptively suggested, the book deals with 'a major theme of the English novel, prominent in Dickens, Forster and Lawrence . . . the theme of the undeveloped heart as it disfigures all relationships, sexual, personal and social, [and] his insights are contemporary, exemplary and developed with extraordinary subtlety.' The accolade is well earned, and it points to Sillitoe's growing stature as a recorder of the contemporary social scene. Now in mid-career, with nine novels, four collections of stories, and respectable work in other genres behind him, he is only beginning to hit his stride as a writer. Already his accomplishments claim our considered attention: that in itself is a good augury for the future.

Notes and References

[1] Reviews quoted in this chapter are listed in the bibliography.
[2] See *The Death of William Posters*, p. 166: 'Myra smiled, though thanked God for the voting Labour masses that still seemed to inhabit the north: cloth-capped, hardworking, generous and bruto, or that was the impression she got from reading a book (or was it books?) called *Hurry on Jim* by Kingsley Wain that started by someone with eighteen pints and fifteen whiskies in him falling downstairs on his way to the top.'

Chapter Eleven

A Summing Up

Britain in the nineteen-fifties was marked by widespread social ferment and dissent. It was a period in which writers being published for the first time frequently voiced their frustration with the complacent leadership of a tradition-bound social and political establishment. Some of the most memorable literary creations of the period were heroic solitaries making their rebellious way through a resisting world, doing their individual best to break up an ossified social structure. Though eloquent indictment of traditional class privilege was not new to English letters, it appeared in the fifties to be more widely debated than ever before. It was in this climate of opinion that Alan Sillitoe's first novel, *Saturday Night and Sunday Morning*, appeared in 1958, followed a year later by *The Loneliness of the Long-Distance Runner*. Although Sillitoe's protagonists in the early fiction fell into a recognisable pattern of dissent, with their proletarian origins, alienated stance and active condemnation of social and political institutions, it was soon seen that they had an additional dimension in their consistent adherence to a class-oriented code of values which gave direction and motive to their actions. Their rejection of the establishment went beyond personal irritation to become an aggressively working-class expression of grievances. They were, in a word, representative. Highly critical of the existing social order and the seemingly unbridgeable gulf between the workers and members of other classes, their incisive commentaries reflected not only the feelings of large numbers of the working class but also the crusading zeal for social reform of Sillitoe himself.

If, as Sillitoe contends, every author is the hero of his own fiction, one is bound to take into account biographical data in order to make sense of the central biases of his work. In his *Notes Towards the Definition of Culture*, T. S. Eliot argued that 'a man should have certain interests and sympathies in common with other men of the same local culture as against those of his own class elsewhere; and interests and sympathies in common with others of his class, irrespective of place.' There can be little doubt that Sillitoe's allegiances lie with the working-class in general and with the milieu of working-class Nottingham in particular, though it would be difficult to 'place' him in any class at the present time. His closeness to the culture he renders in careful detail in the early novels and stories is based directly on the experiences and perceptions of his own life. Born into a working-class family and brought up during the difficult depression years, his outlook was conditioned by the extreme hardship suffered by his own family and others he knew, and by their consequent feelings of resentment and bitterness. Later as a young factory worker he came to understand and sympathise with the social outlook of fellow workers for whom the world was divided into two groups, *them* and *us*.

Walter Davis, who finds a 'striking resemblance' between *Saturday Night and Sunday Morning* and John Lyly's *The Anatomy of Wit*, points to an emphasis in both works on 'the painfulness of experience' and 'the residue of bitter memory, the scars, along with the wisdom it produces'.[1] Sillitoe's personal 'residue of bitter memory' clearly had its effect on his critical perceptions as well as on his fiction. Throughout his essays and commentaries on the work of other writers, at least until the mid-sixties, one finds the consistent thread of a working-class perspective. This is reflected, for example, in his interpretation of the serious artist's two-fold duty: first, that he should concern himself with themes which reflect contemporary social injustice, and second, that he should continually remind his readers of the need for reform. It is also found in the much-quoted *TLS* article, 'Both Sides of the Street', in which he divides writers into two groups. Those of the Right, whom he finds of little value, are content to accept and repeat the values and attitudes of the society they live in. Those of the Left, however, rebel against complacency and evidence of social injustice, and are seen by Sillitoe to be truly creative artists. Novels and stories which reflect this stance are lauded as examples of good literature; those which do not are frequently condemned.

Although excessive reliance on a working-class perspective has lead to a certain myopia in much of Sillitoe's critical writing, his working-class background has been used to better advantage in the fiction. In setting his early work in and around post-war Nottingham, he has used familiar locale, peculiar urban sights, sounds and smells along with patterns of activity in factories, streets and homes to create a fictional working-class world that is firmly anchored in recognisable reality. It is a world marked by a strong sense of communal identity, reflected not only in the characters' intense commitment to neighbourhood life and familiar physical milieu, but also in their subscription to a remarkable number of shared attitudes and assumptions. For most of Sillitoe's working-class characters, life consists in large part of coping with a never-ending series of threats to their peace of mind or physical well-being. While those threats may be real or imagined, they nonetheless carry considerable weight in the characters' perceptions of reality, with the result that the expression of allegiance to their own class is normally defined by expressing antipathy towards the broad spectrum of non-working-class individuals and institutions collectively referred to as *them*. Confrontations with *them*, whether direct or indirect, have a common element: it lies in the sense of persecution which motivates them, a widely-held belief that *they* are pursuing a policy of unjustified enmity and harassment aimed directly against members of the working class. As a result Sillitoe's characters in the early fiction constantly search for ways to redress the balance, to 'get yer own back' in a world dominated by *them*. Principal characters in a number of the Nottingham stories, for example, including Smith in 'The Loneliness of the Long-Distance Runner' and Tony in 'The Ragman's Daughter' feel justified in stealing from *them* and frustrating *their* agents, the police, whenever the opportunity presents itself. Both Arthur Seaton and Liza Atkin in 'The Good Women' support industrial unrest, frustrating the planned-profit formulas of factory owners and bosses. Harold Seaton, along with numerous relatives and others such as Donnie Hodson in 'To Be Collected', rejects and avoids compulsory service in the armed forces. And Brian Seaton devotes a good deal of his energy to castigating past and present power élites and dreaming about the achievement of a new social order.

The rhetoric of insurrection may be found throughout the Nottingham stories, but ironically the characters' concern with the immediate and momentary aspects of perennial confrontation with *them* mitigates against the possibility of their bringing about 'a whole bloody change.' In the Nottingham fiction the lines of battle are clearly drawn, but the characters must content themselves with small triumphs, with temporary and individual successes in skirmishes with *them*. In the first two novels of the trilogy, *The Death of William Posters* and *A Tree on Fire*, Sillitoe's spokesmen for working-class grievances and loyalties would take a more fully-committed stance against various kinds of oppression by *them* in a long-term, sustained attempt to implement the social utopia of their dreams. And in later work the perspective would be altered yet again, with greater emphasis placed on the suffering experienced by particular individuals who had little control over the causes of their distress. In the meantime, belief in the possible achievement of an egalitarian social order and contemplation of revenge against those who control the present one were presented as valuable spiritual resources which Sillitoe's working-class people could draw on to alleviate the physical and psychological pressures afflicting them.

The sensitive middle-class reader, contemplating this presentation of a world with which he is not familiar, might well be expected to question the accuracy with which it is drawn. This is particularly true if the writer is implicitly arguing that a restructuring of society is needed to eliminate the imperfections he is documenting. The reader might ask, for example, whether Sillitoe is misrepresenting working-class perspectives, exaggerating either conditions or attitudes to satisfy some obscure splenetic urge of his own. Fortunately research has clearly shown that Sillitoe's detailed rendering of distressing physical conditions and his mapping of the geography of working-class consciousness are substantially accurate. Documentation underscoring the validity of Sillitoe's representation may be found in a broad range of relevant sociological studies and also in the well-known and eloquent assessment of working-class life by Richard Hoggart, *The Uses of Literacy*.

The *feeling* of accurate representation, as opposed to its proof, is strongly conveyed to the reader of the Nottingham fiction, and most of those who reviewed the work when it first appeared concurred in this assessment. Walter Allen, Frank Kermode and Anthony West, among others, praised the verisimilitude of the early fiction. A number of reviewers were also aware of Sillitoe's political message, some feeling that it played an exacerbated part, especially in *Key to the Door*, while others saw it as potent social indictment. David Caute and Anthony West saw the early fiction in historical perspective, with West forecasting after reading *Saturday Night and Sunday Morning* that 'even if he never writes anything more, he has assured himself a place in the history of the English novel.' West's provocative assertion, that the novel 'breaks new ground' by treating working-class life 'as a normal aspect of the human condition', is based on the premise that for the first time working-class life was being conveyed by a writer 'on the inside looking in.' An examination of the minor, though well-defined tradition of the working-class hero in English fiction, lends support to West's thesis, though at the same time it suggests the need to qualify it. Certainly much working-class fiction from the industrial novels of the 1840's to depression fiction of the 1930's was produced by middle-class writers, often with ill-conceived notions of improving conditions they did not fully comprehend or delineating attitudes they understood imperfectly. An exception must be made in the case of Robert Tressell, who knew intimately the conditions he drew in *The Ragged Trousered Philanthropists* (1914). But Tressell's range was narrow and his characterisation, apart from the novel's protagonist, was unintentional caricature. Sillitoe's personal intimacy with the world he reflects in the Nottingham fiction has resulted in something more substantial, the production of a cohesive group of novels and stories which offer a broadly-based panorama of working-class experience in a world peopled by vital characters linked by shared (and accurately recorded) cultural allegiances and ethical perspectives. To this extent his early work, including *Saturday Night and Sunday Morning*, *The Loneliness of the Long-Distance Runner*, *Key to the Door* and *The Ragman's Daughter*, enrich the tradition of working-class fiction in English, and substantiate West's prescient judgement.

The first two novels of the trilogy, which evoke the Nottingham milieu only in attenuated flashbacks, may be seen to extend the tradition. In *The Death of William Posters* and *A Tree on Fire* the scope is broadened, and the insurrectionary impulse engendered in two men of working-class stock by their sense of social injustice is applied in quite different circumstances from those obtaining in traditional slum settings. Frank Dawley, a restive factory worker, moves outside the confines of the ghetto to forge a new role for himself as a freedom fighter in the battle for Algerian independence. Modifying and building on conventional working-class wisdom, he commits himself fully to the cause of revolution, opening up hitherto unexplored aspects of the long-established tradition of working-class antipathy towards *them*. Albert Handley, the eccentric painter, surrounds himself with the paraphernalia of revolution in his Lincolnshire studio as a stimulus to his work. Motivated by a dual allegiance to his class and to his art, he too builds on the working-class tradition of continual conflict with *them* to preserve his independent perspective. Only in this way, he feels, can he continue to produce provocative art which reveals the evils of a corrupt society and encourages social ferment and revolt. In both *The Death of William Posters* and *A Tree on Fire* Sillitoe was able to transcend his reliance on a detailed chronicle of slum life to sustain the social criticism of his heroes. At the same time he preserved their commitment to the ethical perspectives of working-class life and remained true to his own reformist principles. In work published since 1967, with the special exception of the third novel of the trilogy, *The Flame of Life*, it is clear that Sillitoe has broadened his perspective. The fiction is no longer openly reformist, though in its revelation of the frequently distressing effects of social forces and pressures on suffering individuals, it continues to document the need for serious concern over the drift towards an increasingly dehumanised, conformist society.

Assessments of Sillitoe's talent range from fulminating invective to generous praise. Those who dismiss him usually do so on one of two grounds, either because they are offended by the ungentlemanly conduct of the characters in his early work and by the radical political positions they espouse, or because they find the execution of the work technically flawed. The latter objections, necessarily of greater importance to the discerning reader, are generally concerned with style and narrative technique. Stylistic excesses noted by reviewers of the Nottingham fiction were memorably summed up in Francis Hope's review of *Key to the Door*: 'when Mr Sillitoe tries to decorate his documentary, the metaphors tend to mix, the word-order stumbles, and the far-fetched adjectives pile up in a semantic log-jam.' Reviewers and other critics assessing *The Death of William Posters* and *A Tree on Fire* voiced similar objections to what Frank McGuinness in the *London Magazine* called Sillitoe's indulgent 'weakness for plush prose and imagery' and to 'the self-conscious lyricism of his descriptive passages.' Though enjoyment of verbal decoration is a matter of individual taste, and spare prose is not necessarily a literary virtue, many educated readers are likely to share these reservations about the early work. Objections that some of the longer novels – *Key to the Door*, *The Death of William Posters*, *A Tree on Fire* and *The Flame of Life* – are too loosely constructed and untidy recur in a number of reviews. Certainly these novels have a tendency to sprawl, and one wishes at times that Sillitoe's characters had the ability to define their dilemmas more succinctly and to solve their problems with greater dispatch. Yet this is perhaps to beg the question of the issues' easy resolution: in Sillitoe's fiction the problems persist, the social imperfections remain.

The recognition of a strong didactic element in the early fiction helps the reader to cope with what West called Sillitoe's 'unabashed presence' in the work. It has been argued that such authorial intrusion is unwarranted, that it diminishes the artistic value of his art, but such an argument is open to question. On the one hand it relies too heavily on a purely aesthetic criterion in judging the worth of a piece of literature. That is to say, it comes perilously close to the extreme view 'that art is technique without content – simply a mode of verbal ordering, a decipherable linguistic system that need not be referred back to life or the artist at all.'[2] On the other hand it fails to take into account the peculiar status of working-class fiction in the English literary tradition. This is not to argue that working-class literature should be exempted from rules that are normally applied in the judgement of competent art. It is simply to recognise that working-class life has until recently been largely ignored by creative writers in English, and that when they have found it a fit subject for literature, they have also found that its perennial problems stimulated their consciences as well as their imaginations. In such circumstances distancing becomes difficult, for it runs the risk of blunting the reformist thrust of the art. The thin line between authorial intrusion and ironic detachment is a particularly difficult one for the working-class writer to follow, and Sillitoe has sometimes felt it necessary to intrude. Whether this engagement has inhibited the development of his characters is debateable, but it has certainly not prejudiced their passionate vitality. Still, there are times in the early fiction when one is uneasy at hearing Sillitoe's own professed convictions issuing from the mouths of his characters. In more recent work, of course, this tendency to intrude has been controlled as Sillitoe has moved away from the restricting limitations of a purely working-class perspective.

The fact that Sillitoe devoted most of his output in the first decade of his career to the problems of working-class characters 'pinpoints the rare value' of his work, according to Frank McGuinness: 'Almost alone among English novelists he writes of the ordinary men and women who inhabit those areas of society which affluence may have touched but hardly lit. These are the people who are permanently chained to their dismal birthright ... [unhappily surviving in] a social set-up that can only accommodate them as exploitable units.' While it is true that a number of his contemporaries, including John Braine, Stan Barstow, David Storey and Keith Waterhouse, also produced novels of working-class life, none of them had Sillitoe's commitment to it, nor yet his 'total accord with the milieu and the people' that give his working-class fiction its substance and its range. The nature of his achievement was brought into focus by Bernard Lockwood in an unpublished dissertation when he pointed to E. M. Forster's ironic disclaimer in *Howard's End* (1910): 'We are not concerned with the very poor. They are unthinkable, and only to be approached by the statistician or the poet.' It is largely due to Sillitoe's fictional record of working-class life that Forster's premise is no longer valid. As Lockwood perceptively concluded, the accomplishment of Sillitoe's early work (and to a lesser degree that of his contemporaries) has been to expand the boundaries of English fiction 'so as to include the "unthinkables" as a normal aspect of society and as a natural subject matter for the novelist.'

It is still too early to see Sillitoe's recent work in perspective, though Chapter Ten suggests certain broad trends in the fiction published since 1967. It seems probable that by the late 1960's Sillitoe felt that he had made a comprehensive statement about working-class conditions and aspirations, that he had represented slum living conditions adequately, and that there was little to be gained by repeating accusations of inequality and injustice. As he matured as a writer the demands of his craft began to alter the expression of his principles, with the result that the emphasis in his work shifted. Direct criticism of imperfect institutions and outmoded attitudes, so pervasive in the Nottingham fiction, was pushed into the background by a new focus on the suffering undergone by victims of communal forces and pressures. But the underlying social philosophy remains unaltered. His fiction is still committed to eliminating the benighted views of Josiah Bounderby and his descendants, to creating a world in which human beings of all social ranks can live with dignity and respect.

There will always be readers who find that the attitudes expressed by many of Sillitoe's characters about the nature of modern society are not to their liking, but few will doubt that he is in touch with things that matter. Like Norman Bethune, he believes that

> the function of the artist is to disturb. His duty is to arouse the sleeper, to shake the complacent pillars of the world. He reminds the world of its dark ancestry, shows the world its present, and points the way to its new birth. He is at once the product and the preceptor of his time. After his passage we are troubled and made unsure of our too easily accepted realities. He makes uneasy the static, the set and the still. In a world terrified of change, he preaches revolution – the principle of life. He is an agitator, a disturber of the peace – quick, impatient, positive, restless and disquieting. He is the creative spirit of life working in the soul of men.[3]

Frederick Karl, analysing the writer's role in *The Contemporary English Novel*, echoes Bethune when he tells us that 'when the rebel is authentic and not a poseur he knows that there is little basis for a rapprochement with society. The real protestant is never at rest.' Readers of Sillitoe's fiction are bound to agree. As Robert Taubman wrote in the *Listener* when he reviewed *A Tree on Fire*: 'Alan Sillitoe goes on disturbing.' He could have written it just as easily ten years later about *The Widower's Son*: it is one thing about Sillitoe that is unlikely to change.

Notes and References

[1] Walter R. Davis, *Idea and Act in Elizabethan Fiction*, p. 121.
[2] 'Unreal', editorial, *TLS*, September 4, 1969, p. 976.
[3] Quoted in Sydney Gordon and Ted Allan, *The Scalpel, The Sword*, p. 128.

Selected Bibliography

Books by Alan Sillitoe

Saturday Night and Sunday Morning, W. H. Allen, 1958.
The Loneliness of the Long-Distance Runner, W. H. Allen, 1959.
The General, W. H. Allen, 1960.
The Rats and other poems, W. H. Allen, 1960.
Key to the Door, W. H. Allen, 1961.
The Ragman's Daughter, W. H. Allen, 1963.
A Falling Out of Love and other poems, W. H. Allen, 1964.
Road to Volgograd, W. H. Allen, 1964.
The Death of William Posters, W. H. Allen, 1965.
The City Adventures of Marmalade Jim, Macmillan, 1967.
A Tree on Fire, Macmillan, 1967.
Guzman, Go Home, Macmillan, 1968.
Love in the Environs of Voronezh and other poems, Macmillan, 1968.
A Start in Life, W. H. Allen, 1970.
Travels in Nihilon, W. H. Allen, 1971.
Raw Material, W. H. Allen, 1972.
Men, Women and Children, W. H. Allen, 1973.
The Flame of Life, W. H. Allen, 1974.
Storm: new poems, W. H. Allen, 1974.
Mountains and Caverns, W. H. Allen, 1975.
The Widower's Son, W. H. Allen, 1976.
Big John and the Stars, Robson Books, 1977.
The Incredible Fencing Fleas, Robson Books, 1978.
Three Plays, W. H. Allen, 1978.

Articles by Alan Sillitoe

'Arnold Bennett: The Man from the North', Introduction to Bennett's *The Old Wives' Tale*, London: Pan, 1964.

'Books You Can Never Escape', *Off the Shelf: A Library Guide at Home and at School*, London: Macmillan, 1967, pp. 72–3.

'Both Sides of the Street', *Times Literary Supplement*, July 8, 1960, p. 435.

'Dead Caucus of English Prose', *Books and Bookmen*, February 1960, p. 5.

'Drilling and Burring', *Spectator*, January 3, 1964, pp. 11–12.

'An Exhilarating Start', *Bookman*, January–February 1960, p. 3.

'I Reminded Him of Muggleton', *Shanendoah*, 13 No. 2 (1962), pp. 49–54.

'Introduction' to Robert Tressell's *The Ragged Trousered Philanthropists*, London: Panther, 1965.

'Introduction' to *Saturday Night and Sunday Morning*, London: Longmans, 1968.

'Introduction' to *A Sillitoe Selection*, London: Longmans, 1968.

'Johnny Livens Up Grim Schooldays', *Reynolds News*, January 31, 1960, p. 11.

'My Israel', *New Statesman*, December 20, 1974, pp. 890–92.

'Nightmare of War by a Deserter', *Reynolds News*, February 7, 1960, p. 11.

'Novel or Play?' *Twentieth Century*, 169 (1961), 206–11.

'Orwell's First Novel', *Guardian*, May 13, 1960, p. 7.

'The Pen Was My Enemy', *Books and Bookmen*, January 1959, p. 11.

'Poor People', *Anarchy*, 38 (April 1964), pp. 124–8.

'Portrait of Robert Graves', *Books and Bookmen*, May 1960, pp. 7–8.

'Proletarian Novelists', *Books and Bookmen*, August 1959, p. 13.

'Strictly Personal', *Education*, October 14, 1960, 678–9.

'Symposium (interview)', *Penthouse*, March 1965, pp. 12–24, 68–9.

'Through Five Centuries with Priestley', *Reynolds News*, February 14, 1960, p. 7.

'Through the Tunnel', *World Marxist Review*, 8, No. 1 (1965), pp. 23–5.

Untitled article. *Sixth form opinion*, 7 (1963), 25.

Untitled review of *Gangrene*, ed. Peter Benenson, *Books and Bookmen*, December 1959, p. 37.

Untitled review of *Weekend in Dinlock* by Clancy Segal, *Bookman*, December 1959, p. 3.

'Voltaire and the Calas Case', *Listener*, July 27, 1961, pp. 144–5.

'What Comes on Monday?' *New Left Review*, 4 (July–August 1960), 58–9.

'When will the Russians see that humanity is good for them?' *The Times*, June 10, 1974, p. 14.

Published Material Quoted

Allen, Walter, 'In the World of the Bottom Dogs', *New York Times Book Review*, March 25, 1962, p. 5.

Altick, Richard, *The Art of Literary Research*, rev. ed. New York: Norton, 1975.

Anon. 'Blessings in Disguise', *Times Literary Supplement* (hereafter cited as *TLS*) November 7, 1958, p. 646.

—— 'Book Review', *London Magazine*, March 1960, pp. 65–6.

—— 'Book Review', *Time*, April 18, 1960, pp. 74–5.

—— 'Notes on Current Books', *Virginia Quarterly Review*, 40, No. 2 (1964), lx.

—— 'Books', *Nottingham Evening Post*, October 17, 1958, p. 6.

—— 'Borstal and Cambridge', *TLS*, October 2, 1959, p. 557.

—— 'Fiction Round-up', *The Times*, December 21, 1968, p. 19.

—— 'Love and War', *TLS*, October 24, 1968, p. 1193.

—— 'New Fiction', *The Times*, October 8, 1959, p. 15.

—— 'New Fiction', *The Times*, October 19, 1961, p. 15.

—— 'Nothing Doing', *TLS*, September 17, 1971, p. 1105.

—— 'Nottingham theme of local writer's first novel', *Guardian Journal*, October 13, 1958, p. 4.

—— 'Scenes From Provincial Life', *TLS*, October 20, 1961, p. 749.

—— 'Short But Strong', *TLS*, October 18, 1963, p. 821.

—— 'Short Stories', *The Times*, October 17, 1963, p. 15.

—— 'Symbolism must merge with Realism, says Alan Sillitoe', *Books and Bookmen*, October 1961, pp. 7–8.

—— 'Unreal', editorial, *TLS*, September 4, 1969, p. 976.

—— Untitled review, *The Times*, May 13, 1965, p. 15.

—— 'Working Class Novelist', *Books and Bookmen*, October 1958, p. 16.

Baro, Gene, 'A New Impressive Talent', *New York Herald Tribune Book Review*, April 8, 1962, pp. 6–7.

—— 'Tales of British Working Class Life', *New York Herald Tribune Book Review*, May 29, 1960, p. 6.

—— 'Book Review', *New York Herald Tribune Books*, April 8, 1962, pp. 6–7.

Barrett, William, 'Reader's Choice', *Atlantic*, May 1962, pp. 122–4.

Berrie, John, 'Book With a Real Nottingham Accent', *Nottingham Evening Post*, September 25, 1959, p. 4.

Bethune, Norman, 'An Apology for Not Writing Letters', quoted in Sydney Gordon and Ted Allan, *The Scalpel, The Sword*, London: Robert Hale, 1954, p. 128.

Booth, Wayne, 'Yes, But Are They Really Novels?' *Yale Review*, June 1962, pp. 634–5.

Boroff, David, 'Glimpses of a Shabby Gaiety', *Saturday Review*, April 16, 1960, p. 27.

Bowen, John. 'What Is There New to Learn From the View of "Them" and "Us"?' *New York Times Book Review*, January 12, 1964, pp. 4–5.

Bradbury, Malcolm, 'Beating the World to the Punch', *New York Times Book Review*, August 16, 1959, pp. 4–5.

—— 'Beneath the Veneer, Pure Animal Life', *New York Times Book Review*, April 10, 1960, p. 5.

—— 'New Fiction', *Punch*, November 8, 1961, p. 696.

Bragg, Melvyn, 'Class and the Novel', *TLS*, October 15, 1971, p. 1262.

Braine, John, 'Lunch with J. B. Priestley', *Encounter*, June 1958, pp. 8–14.

—— *Room at the Top*, London: Spottiswoode, 1957.

Brand, C. F., *The British Labour Party*, London: Oxford University Press, 1965.

Calder, Robert L., *W. Somerset Maugham and the Quest for Freedom*, London: Heinemann, 1972.

Callaghan, Barry, 'The world of a terrified child', [Toronto] *Telegram*, October 26, 1968, p. 5.

Caute, David, 'Breakthrough', *Time and Tide*, October 12, 1961, p. 1705.

Churchill, Randolph S., *Winston S. Churchill*, 2 vols. London: Heinemann, 1967.

Cole, G. D. H., *The Post War Condition of Britain*, London: Routledge and Kegan Paul, 1956.

Cole, G. D. H. and Raymond Postgate, *The Common People 1746–1946*, 4th ed., 1949; rev. London: Methuen, 1961.

Coleman, John, 'On the Run', *Observer*, May 9, 1965, p. 26.

—— 'Resign the Living', *Spectator*, September 25, 1959, p. 416.

—— 'The Unthinkables', *New Statesman*, October 27, 1961, pp. 610, 612.

Connolly, Cyril. 'Mild-and-Bitter Rebel', *Sunday Times*, October 15, 1961, p. 31.

Coustillas, Pierre and Colin Partridge, eds, *Gissing: The Critical Heritage*, London: Routledge and Kegan Paul, 1972.

Crosland, Anthony, 'Smashing Things', *Spectator*, 204 (February 12, 1960), p. 223.

Dalton, Hugh, *High Tide and After: Memoirs 1945–1960*, London: Frederick Muller, 1962.

Davenport, John, 'Leaden Days of Youth', *Observer*, October 15, 1961, p. 29.

Davies, Russell, 'Doomed to success', *Observer*, November 28, 1976, p. 30.

Davis, Walter R., *Idea and Act in Elizabethan Fiction*, Princeton: The University Press, 1969.

Dennis, Norman et al., *Coal is our Life: An Analysis of a Yorkshire Mining Community*, London: Tavistock, 1959.

Dickens, Charles, *Hard Times*, 1854; rpt. Harmondsworth, Middlesex: Penguin, 1970.

Disraeli, Benjamin, *Sybil or The Two Nations*, 1845; rpt. London: Thomas Nelson & Sons, 1957.

Dobbs, Kildare, *Reading the Time*, Toronto: Macmillan, 1968.

Downes, David M., *The Delinquent Solution: A Study in Subcultural Theory*, London: Routledge and Kegan Paul, 1968.

Eliot, George, *Felix Holt: The Radical*, 1886; rpt. Harmondsworth, Middlesex: Penguin, 1972.

Eliot, T. S., *Notes Towards the Definition of Culture*, London: Faber and Faber, 1948.

Fraser, G. S., *The Modern Writer and His World*, London: Andre Deutsch, 1964.

Fuller, John, 'New Novels', *Listener*, October 19, 1961, p. 621.

Furbank, P. N., 'Rags to Riches', *Encounter*, February 1964, pp. 81–2.

Fyvel, T. R., *The Insecure Offenders: Rebellious Youth in the Welfare State*, London: Chatto and Windus, 1961.

Gaskell, Elizabeth, *Mary Barton*, 1848; rpt. Harmondsworth, Middlesex: Penguin, 1970.

—— *North and South*, 1855; rpt. London: Oxford University Press, 1977.

Gindin, James, *Postwar British Fiction: New Accents and Attitudes*, Berkeley: University of California Press, 1962.

Gissing, George, *Demos*, 1886; rpt. ed. Pierre Coustillas, Hassocks, Sussex: Harvester Press, 1974.

—— *The Nether World*, 1889; rpt. London: Dent (Everyman), 1974.

Glanville, Brian, 'Bread and Cocoa Memories for Alan Sillitoe', *Reynolds News*, December 7, 1958, p. 6.

Glicksberg, Charles I, *The Self in Modern Literature*, University Park, Pennsylvania: Penn State University Press, 1962.

Green, Henry, *Living*, 1929; rpt. London: Pan Books (Picador), 1978 (with *Loving* and *Party Going* in one volume).

Green, Peter, 'Book Review', *Daily Telegraph and Morning Post*, October 17, 1958, p. 15.

Greenwood, Walter, *Love on the Dole*, 1933; rpt. Harmondsworth, Middlesex: Penguin, 1969.

Hanley, James, *The Furys*, 1935; rpt. Bath: Lythway Press, 1974.

—— *The Secret Journey*, 1936; rpt. Bath: Lythway Press, 1974.

Hardy, Barbara, *The Novels of George Eliot*, London: Athlone Press, 1959.

Heasman, D. J., ' "My Station and Its Duties" – The Attlee Version', *Parliamentary Affairs*, 21 (Winter 1967–68), pp. 75–84.

Hilton, Frank, 'Britain's New Class', *Encounter*, February 1958, pp. 59–63.

Hoggart, Richard, *The Uses of Literacy: Aspects of working-class life with special reference to publications and entertainments*, London: Chatto and Windus, 1957.

Hope, Francis, 'Novels', *Encounter*, December 1961, pp. 75–6.

Hough, Graham, 'New Novels', *Listener*, October 1, 1959, p. 542.

Howe, Irving, 'The Worker As A Young Tough', *New Republic*, August 24, 1958, pp. 27–8.

—— 'In Fear of Thinking' *New Republic*, May 28, 1962, pp. 25–6.

Hynes, Samuel, 'A Quality of Honesty', *Commonweal*, April 6, 1962, p. 46.

Jackson, Brian, *Working-Class Community: Some general notions raised by a series of studies in northern England*, New York: Praeger, 1968.

James, Louis, *Fiction for the Working Man 1830–1850*, London: Oxford University Press, 1963.

Jebb, Julian, 'Book Review', *Sunday Times*, November 3, 1963, p. 37.

Jenkins, Sarah, 'The Man Who Made Me Forget My Hard Chair', *News Chronicle*, January 16, 1960, p. 3.

Johnson, Pamela Hansford, 'New Novels', *New Statesman*, October 3, 1959, p. 448.

Jones, D. A. N., 'Regimental disorders', *TLS*, November 26, 1976, p. 1473.

Karl, Frederick R., *The Contemporary English Novel*, New York: Farrar, Strauss, and Cudahy, 1962.

Keating, P. J., *The working classes in Victorian fiction*, London: Routledge and Kegan Paul, 1971.

Kermode, Frank, 'Fiction Chronicle', *Partisan Review*, 29 (1962), pp. 634-5.

—— 'Rammel', *New Statesman*, May 14, 1965, pp. 765-6.

Kerr, Madeline, *The People of Ship Street*, London: Routledge and Kegan Paul, 1958.

Kettle, Arnold, 'Book Review', *Daily Worker*, October 16, 1961, p. 2.

Kingsley, Charles, *Alton Locke*, 1850; rpt. London: Dent (Everyman), 1970.

Koningsberger, Hans, 'Dropped Aitches in Malaya', *Saturday Review*, March 24, 1962, p. 26.

Lask, Thomas, 'Nobody Throws In The White Towel', *New York Times*, January 15, 1964, p. 29.

Lawrence, D. H., *Selected Essays*, Harmondsworth, Middlesex: Penguin, 1950.

Lee, James W., *John Braine*, New York: Twayne, 1968.

Levine, Paul, 'Some Middle-Aged Fiction', *The Hudson Review* 18 (1965-66), pp. 590-1.

Maison, Margaret, Untitled essay, *Observer*, December 27, 1963, p. 3.

Martin, John M., *Juvenile Vandalism: A Study of its Nature and Prevention*, Springfield, Illinois: Charles C. Thomas, 1961.

Mayne, Richard, 'Book Review', *Sunday Times*, October 12, 1958, p. 18.

Mays, John, *Growing Up in the City: A Study of Juvenile*

Delinquency in an Urban Neighbourhood, Liverpool: University Press, 1954.

McCallum, R. B. and Alison Readman, *The British General Election of 1945*, London: Oxford University Press, 1947.

McGuinness, Frank, 'Selected Books', *London Magazine*, August 1965, pp. 102–104.

McMichael, George, 'Book Review', *San Francisco Sunday Chronicle*, March 27, 1962, p. 29.

Miller, Karl, 'Sillitoe and Son', *New Statesman*, October 18, 1963, p. 530.

Moynahan, Julian, 'Alan Sillitoe at Midpoint', *New York Times Book Review*, July 24, 1977, pp. 1, 21–2.

Moon, Eric, 'Against the Establishment', *Saturday Review*, August 21, 1965, p. 27.

—— 'Fiction', *Library Journal*, February 15, 1962, p. 786.

—— 'Pegasus in the Grime', *Saturday Review*, January 25, 1964, p. 39.

Morrison, Arthur, *Tales of Mean Streets*, 1894; rpt. London: Methuen, 1912.

—— *A Child of the Jago*, 1896; rpt. ed. P. J. Keating, London: MacGibbon and Kee, 1969.

—— *To London Town*, London: Methuen, 1899.

Mortimer, Penelope, 'A Remarkable Achievement', *Bookman*, September 1959, p. 11.

Mumford, Lewis, *The Culture of Cities*, New York: Harcourt, Brace, 1938.

O'Connor, William Van, *The New University Wits*, Carbondale: South Illinois University Press, 1963.

Orwell, George, *The Road to Wigan Pier*, 1937; rpt. Harmondsworth, Middlesex: Penguin, 1970.

Pelling, Henry, *A Short History of the Labour Party*, London: Macmillan, 1962.

Penner, Allen, *Alan Sillitoe*, New York: Twayne, 1972.

Perrott, Roy, 'Miss Murdoch rings the bell', *Manchester Guardian*, November 4, 1958, p. 6.

—— 'Life through the eyes of the odd man out', *Guardian*, September 25, 1959, p. 7.

Potter, Dennis, *The Glittering Coffin*, London: Victor Gollancz, 1960.

Price, R. G. G., 'New Fiction', *Punch*, October 14, 1959, p. 315.

Priestley, J. B., *The Good Companions*, London: Heinemann, 1929.

Raven, Simon, 'Two Kinds of Jungle', *Spectator*, October 20, 1961, p. 555.

Read, Donald, *The English Provinces c. 1760–1960: A Study in Influence*, London: Edward Arnold, 1964.

Richardson, Maurice, 'New Novels', *New Statesman*, October 18, 1958, pp. 539–40.

—— 'Bores and super-bores', *Observer*, December 1, 1974, p. 34.

Richler, Mordecai, 'Proles on Parade', *Spectator*, October 25, 1963, p. 535.

Roberts, Robert, *The Classic Slum: Salford Life in the first quarter of the century*, Manchester: University Press, 1971.

Rutherford, Mark, pseud. William Hale White, *The Revolution in Tanner's Lane*, 1887; rpt. London: Oxford University Press, 1936.

Spark, Muriel, 'Borstal Boy', *Observer*, October 11, 1959, p. 21.

Spinley, B. M., *The Deprived and the Privileged: Personality Development in English Society*, London: Routledge and Kegan Paul, 1953.

Storey, David, 'Which Revolution?' *Guardian*, October 18, 1963, p. 6.

Taubman, Robert, 'Empty England', *Listener*, November 9, 1967, p. 610.

Tawney, R. H., *Equality*, London: George Allen and Unwin, 1931.

Totten, Nick, 'Craftsmen', *Spectator*, November 27, 1976, pp. 30–31.

Townsend, John, *The Young Devils: Experiences of a School-Teacher*, London: Chatto and Windus, 1958.

Tressell, Robert, pseud. Robert Noonan, *The Ragged*

Trousered Philanthropists, 1914; rpt. London: Panther, 1965.

Updike, John, 'Voices from Downtroddendom', *New Republic*, May 9, 1960, pp. 11–12.

Wain, John, 'Possible Worlds', *Observer*, October 12, 1958, p. 20.

Wardle, Irving, 'Return of the Prodigal', *Observer*, October 13, 1963, p. 24.

Watt, Ian, *The Rise of the Novel: Studies in Defoe, Richardson, and Fielding*, London: Chatto and Windus, 1957.

Wells, Dee, 'One Boy's Private War', *Sunday Express*, September 20, 1959, p. 6.

West, Anthony, 'On the Inside Looking In', *New Yorker*, September 5, 1959, pp. 99–100.

—— 'Puppets and People', *New Yorker*, June 11, 1960, pp. 145–6.

Williams, Raymond, *Culture and Society 1780–1950*, London: Chatto and Windus, 1958.

Yaffe, James, 'Book Review', *Saturday Review*, September 5, 1959, p. 17.

Young, Michael, *The Rise of the Meritocracy 1870–2033: An Essay on Educational Equality*, Harmondsworth, Middlesex: Penguin, 1958.

Young, Michael and Peter Willmott, *Family and Kinship in East London*, London: Routledge and Kegan Paul, 1957.

Zweig, Ferdynand, *The British Worker*, Harmondsworth, Middlesex: Penguin, 1952.

—— *Labour, Life and Poverty*, London: Gollancz, 1948.

Unpublished Material Quoted

Burns, Johnnie Wade, 'An Examination of Elements of Socialist Realism in Five Novels of Alan Sillitoe.' Unpublished dissertation, George Peabody College for Teachers, 1975.

Dobbs, Kildare, 'The Sounds of Criticism.' An essay for radio, presented on the Canadian Broadcasting Corporation's FM Network between March 18 and April 15, 1966.

Gilbert, B. A., 'Alan Sillitoe: A Conflicting Temperament.'
Unpublished dissertation, Bordeaux University, 1965.

Lockwood, Bernard, 'Four Contemporary British Novelists:
A Thematic and Critical Approach to the Fiction of
Raymond Williams, John Braine, David Storey, and
Alan Sillitoe.' Unpublished dissertation, University of
Wisconsin, 1967.

Sillitoe, Alan, MS. 'Arnold Bennett.' Speech given at Stoke-
on-Trent, May 27, 1965, 6 pp.

—— MS. 'Chance Reading.' London: n.d., 5 pp.

—— MS. 'Hawthornden Award Speech.' London: June
1960, 5 pp.